DAY TRADING FOR BEGINNERS

The Complete Guide With Day Trading Options Techniques And Strategies

By

George Livermore

AF677569

This document is geared in the direction of giving precise and also trustworthy info when it comes to the subject and concern covered. The publication is offered with the concept that the author is not required to make accountancy, formally allowed, or otherwise qualified services. If advice is required, lawful, or specialist, a practiced individual in the profession should be gotten.

From a Statement of Concepts that was accepted and accepted similarly by a Board of the American Bar Organization and a Board of Publishers and Associations, in no way is it legal to duplicate, duplicate, or send any part of this record in either electronic means or in printed format. Recording of this magazine is strictly forbidden, and also any type of storage space of this file is not allowed

of the details is without agreement or any type of kind of guarantee assurance.

The hallmarks that are made use of are without any authorization, as well as the magazine of the hallmark lacks authorization or backing by the trademark owner. All trademarks, as well as brands within this publication, are for clarifying objectives just and also are possessed by the proprietors themselves, not affiliated with this document.

Table of Contents

INTRODUCTION

Day trading is not betting or a pastime. I wake up early, go for a run, take a shower, get dressed, consume breakfast, and fire up my trading station prior to the markets open in New York. I am inspired when I sit down and begin working on the list of stocks I will view that day.

For newbie traders, this book offers you an understanding of where to begin, how to begin, what to anticipate from day trading, and how to establish your method. Earnings in trading do not come with checking out a book or two or searching online.

Day trading, as the name suggests, is when you purchase and offer monetary investments throughout the day and clear your impressive trades prior to you close the marketplace. The main goal is to make fast benefit from any cost boost or reduce that occurs on a single trading day.

When the stock exchange opens, any news that is launched in the future might bring the opening cost of a monetary instrument on the next trading day. From a tactical perspective, day trading decreases the threat of sustaining losses overnight due to distinctions in between the opening cost and the closing rate of the previous day. Stocks, currencies, shares, and futures are the most actively traded monetary instruments of the day.

In the book, I explain the principles of day trading, describe how day trading is various from other designs of trading and financial investment, and elaborate on crucial trading techniques that numerous traders utilize every day. I've kept the book brief so you can, in fact, end up reading it and not get tired by the middle.

WHAT IS DAY TRADING?

Day trading is a great option to gain your financial freedom in a short time.

If you're brand-new to trading, keep reading since this chapter is a little guide to describe precisely what the day of trading is.

Day trading is a wild, exciting, and often exhausting business. When you should be a day trader, so you need to be willing to make fast choices.

You need to likewise make sure when dealing since there will be absolutely nothing rewarding to purchase for some days, and it will appear to others that whatever is losing cash, and being is a crucial ability.

You may desire to discover a part-time trading position if you're looking to make additional money without devoting to trading complete time. Now, this doesn't mean you should go-go trading when you don't have much else to do, and it's always necessary to insist on taking 100 per cent Effort any time you purchase, even though you don't have the faith you'll lose cash at the end of the day.

How Day Trading Works

How does Day Trading work? As Robert Deel keeps in mind, the meaning of a day trader is somebody who goes into the marketplace eventually throughout the day and is completely in money by the end of the day. At no time does a day trader bring a position overnight.

It is needed for you to select the ideal timing of entering into and bailing out of the stock for taking advantage of short-term investing. This is how all the procedure works.

Prior to beginning share investing through online financial investment companies, you ought to collect concrete info on the variety of dissatisfied and pleased client of the business. Such details are quickly readily available for the consumer to utilize any share brokerage company. The company without such info or declining to offer them ought to be prevented as they may posture severe danger in the future.

With the share financial investment being technologized, some companies declare for having actually made great amount through traders from the choices and pointers they supplied to them. Once again, you must choose to decline and having an extensive search to choose the info that these online trading companies offer to you.

You may want riding momentum of any stock and bail out prior to the twist in turn. Specialists feel that it is in some cases, much better for selecting blended methods while investing in brief term stocks.

For people who are searching for techniques while getting associated with such a design of share investing, they need to safeguard themselves from the possible negatives of the trading.

Day Trading generally includes considerable time financial investments, as day-to-day changes tend to show market beliefs instead of the real efficiency of the underlying stock. Day traders often count on chart patterns to time their relocations - one chart pattern that is frequently thought about extremely important is the bearish engulf, where an uptrend is totally swallowed up by a sag; this suggests a coming high drop-in rate.

The traders have lots of alternatives like the modern-day online trading or the traditional where one purchases and offers their shares being at the stock exchange. It must be kept in mind that modern-day approaches are far way ahead of the traditional methods as they work at a quick rate within the course of a day.

Traders are the 'quick amount' individuals, and they are typically having the affinity for getting swayed by the big talks of marketers and little brokers. Here, they can constantly get caught in a risk. A knowledgeable stockbroker constantly recommends preventing the claims of ads assuring fast and guaranteed gains through trading.

As a typical situation with all online and routine stockbroker dealerships, a financial investment company requires to have registration with the governing body of your location. As these types of companies are incredibly dangerous, the traders frequently lack wealth endurance and time required to make cash.

These stock financiers are needed to pay the companies with the ideas and time that their authorities supply. These brokerage companies start with their making procedure from the time you go into the company unimportant of the scenario of your financial investment.

Scalpers

This kind of day trader trades for portions of a point. This method is extremely emotionally requiring and has a high rate of failure. Prior to you choose to end up being a scalper, keep in mind the stats: 92 per cent of scalpers lose cash.

Traders in intraday trend This sort of day trader persists in a deal until the trend reverses. This could take anywhere from a couple of minutes to a number of hours, depending on the marketplace.

Day trading usually needs a significant amount of operating money. Generally, you will need a total of $50,000 to be able to cover the selling fees (brokerage fees, clearance costs, etc.).

Microtrend traders

Microtrend traders, unlike day traders, typically keep trading for 3 to 5 days. We seek to sell a portion of a larger plan, then use stops if the planned trend reverses tremendously to deter the merchant from a deal. Successful micro trend trading requires the entry to be made at a point where the pattern is solid, preferably when explosively begins.

Micro trend trading is normally less demanding than day trading. Micro trend trading likewise needs less capital in order to achieve success.

Position pattern trader

How to day trade like a position pattern trader? Position pattern traders try to ride patterns for at least 5days.

The quantity of capital needed for position pattern trading differs; usually, the minimum quantity required for success to be lower than that for microtrend trading and day trading.

What Are The Benefits

The two significant advantages of day trading are fast exit to losses and instant outcomes. Day trading forces a fast trade of a losing stock which keeps the shareholder from sitting it out to see if the stock increases. Moreover, instant outcomes can assist a trader in tightening their abilities and assisting them in ending up being a more effective trader.

Day trading is the procedure of purchasing a stock and offering it in the very same day. An individual is thought about a day trader when they finish four or more day trades in a five company day duration and has two unmet day trade calls in 90 days.

Day trading is seen by some as a fantastic ability that is the only method to play the stock video game. Day trading does use numerous advantages, and maybe it is the advantages that draw so lots of to the concept of day trading

Day trading can be helpful for some individuals and not so for others. The option depends on the trader. The threats and advantages must be thoroughly weighed and the choice made upon an informed understanding of day trading.

In addition to possibly huge earnings, day trading has numerous advantages for those unusual people who can handle their feelings and hold up against the intrinsic pressures:

Due to the reality that there are so numerous more sellers and purchasers utilizing Currency day trading than buying in the capital exchange would still be open to those willing to sell when the time arrives. They can always appreciate the fact that investing on a currency day is easier than selling in the stock exchange because of the huge amount it deals with every day.

With futures, that very same margin might manage you the capability to trade a much bigger notional worth.

Another fantastic advantage is being able to trade twenty-four hours a day, five days a week. Another thing that makes currency day trading so enticing is the reality that you just require to put up a portion of the capital needed when making a trade rather of the entire quantity upfront.

Regardless of the advantages, day traders need to handle a variety of mental and monetary dangers:

Capital Loss. Even if a bulk of trades pay, substantial up-front expenses such as hardware, software application, and preliminary news services should be paid prior to one can start trading. Continuous costs such as ECN charges (or commissions if the trader is not utilizing an ECN), interest, real-time news charges, monetary analysis and charting bundles, and interaction charges should be preserved.

Michael Sincere, day trader and author of "Start Day Trading Now," declares it is difficult to make cash when the market moves less than 100 points in either instruction from the day previously. Too lots of traders are going after to a couple of chances, indicating that just those fast adequate to acknowledge a chance and act are most likely to make cash.

Mental Addiction. According to Ed Looney, executive director of the Council on Compulsive Gambling of New Jersey, day trading is "like fracture drug, and it's a lot more addictive than another sort of betting." Some psychologists recommend that bettors and day traders are comparable because they tend to be competitive and of above-average intelligence.

As an equity trader, have you ever been locked out of trading due to a day trading infraction? Or have you missed out on a chance due to brief selling constraints?

Missed out on chances can be pricey, so we will take a look at a few of the constraints in the United States for day trading money equity items and compare that today trading with futures.

In contrast, a futures trader does not have the very same brief sale constraints. You can take a brief position as quickly as a long position.

Self-reliance. Lots of day traders are self-employed, working on their own and answerable to nobody. They hold true business owners living by their wits and, ideally, profiting off their own choices.

Bliss. There are a couple of occasions that can match the psychological high that features a substantial revenue made exclusively by the efforts of a bachelor.

Status. Day traders inhabit a practically legendary status in specific neighbourhoods, comparable in numerous methods to the famous "quick weapons" of the old West-- renowned outsiders living by their own guidelines and making their own method.

Minimum Account Size

A pattern day trader who performs four or more round turns in single security within a week is needed to preserve minimum equity of $25,000 in their brokerage account.

A futures trader is not needed to fulfil this minimum account size. As long as you preserve the minimum margin requirements for your positions, you can trade as often as you like at a size ideal to your trading requirements.

No Short Sale Restrictions

Another typical battle for equity day traders is that in order to short security, there should be shares readily available to trade. And there are numerous reasons shares might not be readily available.

You will discover that there are numerous advantages to currency day trading if you have the time and clients to discover as much as you can about utilizing the system. Make an effort to do your research study and discover whatever possible about the fundamentals of this type of trading and then browse for the system that works finest for your requirements.

It has a lot of advantages to use modern-day financier. One of the greatest advantages of currency day trading is the reality that you are not restricted to just trading shares you can likewise invest in currency, home and products. You have more range which offers you the chance to make more cash with your financial investments.

Minimum Tick

When a trader shorts a stock, they are needed to cost a minimum of a tick above last traded cost. This indicates in a down-trending market, an, and an equity trader might never ever get to take a brief position, hence losing on a market chance. Futures trader can be brief the market simply as quickly as being long.

Margin

An equity trader can just trade as much as four times their upkeep margin excess on an intra-day basis. If they have $30,000 upkeep excess offered, they can just trade up to a worth of $120,000. Surpass this quantity and margin calls might even more restrict purchasing power and trading frequency.

DAY TRADING WITH OPTIONS OR WITH SHARES- WHAT IS THE DIFFERENCE?

Everybody understands that purchasing something now and offering it later on at a greater cost is the course to earnings. That is not great enough for alternatives traders since alternative costs do not constantly act as anticipated, and this space in understanding might trigger traders to leave cash on the table or sustain unforeseen losses.

Among the significant problems for brand-new choices, traders develop originates from them not truly comprehending how to utilize alternatives to achieve their monetary objectives since alternatives trade in a different way than stocks.

Whether you are a financier or a trader, your goal is to generate income. Your secondary goal is to do so with the appropriate minimum level of threat.

Choices are unique financial investment tools, and there is far more a trader can do than merely purchase and offer specific choices. Choices have qualities that are not readily available somewhere else in the financial investment universe.

Binary alternatives traders "gamble" on whether or not a possession's rate will be above or listed below a particular quantity at a defined time. Day traders likewise try to forecast cost instructions. However, losses and revenues depend on elements like entry rate, exit rate, size of the trade, and cash management methods. Like binary choices traders, day traders can go into a trade understanding the optimum gain or loss by utilizing revenue targets and stop losses.

An alternative is a monetary derivative that offers the holder the right, however not the commitment, to either purchase or offer a set quantity of a security or other monetary property at an agreed-upon cost (the strike cost) on or prior to a defined date. A binary alternative, nevertheless, instantly workouts, so the holder does not have the option to purchase or offer the hidden possession.

A binary choice is a type of choices in which your profit/loss depends totally on the result of a yes/no market proposal: a binary alternatives trader will either make a set loss or a set revenue. Revenue or loss for a day trader relies on a variety of factors, comprising of entrance rate, departure expense, and amount of securities, deals, or lots sold and bought by the dealer.

The Greeks Statistical Methods Professional commodity traders don't buy stock all the time. For certain situations, they appreciate giving brief wanting to profit as the cost of product declines. A lot of beginner alternative traders do rule out the principle of offering alternatives (hedged to restrict threat), instead of purchasing them.

Binary choices are offered on a range of underlying properties, consisting of stocks, products, currencies, indices and even occasions, such as an approaching Fed Funds Rate, Jobless Claims and Nonfarm Payrolls statements. An alternative binary position a yes/no concern: for example, Will the cost of gold be above $1,326 at 1:30 p.m.? The cost at which you purchase or offer the binary alternative is not the real cost of gold (in this example) however a worth in between absolutely no and 100.

If you can determine danger (i.e., optimum gain or loss) for a provided position, then you can likewise lessen it. Translation: Traders can prevent nasty surprises by understanding just how much cash can be lost when the worst-case circumstance takes place.

Traders should understand the possible benefit for any position in order to identify whether looking for that possible benefit is worth the threat needed.

A couple of elements that alternatives traders utilize to assess risk/reward capacity:

Holding a position for a particular time period. Unlike stock, all alternatives decline as time passes. The Greek letter "Theta" is utilized to explain how the passage of one day impacts the worth of choice.

Delta determines how a cost modification, either greater or lower, for underlying stock or index impacts the rate of choice.

She continued to cost modification. That is another method of stating that the choice Delta is not consistent, however modifications.

It is extremely various for stock (no matter the stock cost, the worth of one share of stock constantly alters by $1 when the stock rate modifications by $1), and the idea is something with which a brand-new choices trader should be comfy.

In the world of choice, altering volatility plays a big function in the prices of the alternatives. Vega determines how much the cost of alternative modifications when approximated volatility modifications.

Hedging with Spreads

Choices are typically utilized in mix with other alternatives (i.e., purchase one and offer another). That might sound complicated. However, the basic concept is easy: When you have an expectation for the hidden property habits, such as:

Technical Analysis vs Fundamental Analysis.

Generally, day traders are more interested in a stock's cost action, whereas financiers are more focused on the underlying business. Day traders might likewise use take advantage of for a greater concentration of shares to pocket a smaller sized relative rate motion rate gain.

Commissions.

A day trader could get several times in a single day into and out of a position, while the financiers could keep positions for years or months. Contrary to this, day traders often move in and out of roles and profits will quickly add rising.

- ✓ Bearish
- ✓ Neutral (anticipating a range-bound market).
- ✓ It is ending up being far more, or much less, unstable.

The number of possible mixes is big, and you can discover info on a range of choices techniques that utilize spreads. In exchange for accepting restricted earnings, spread out trading comes with its own benefits, such as a boosted likelihood of making cash. Stock traders have absolutely nothing comparable to choice spreads.

Choices trading is not stock trading. For the informed choice trader, that is an advantage due to the fact that choice methods can be developed to make money from a variety of stock exchange results, which can be achieved with minimal danger.

Contrary to this, financiers are based on large industry: industry this they believe can expand in the years to come. Although uncertainty is beneficial to a day trader, to a financier, it may reflect chaos. Financiers tend to search for much safer stocks from the more genuine business.

Threat Exposure.

Drawback danger can form from global markets and occasions while U.S. stock exchange is closed, leading to futures gapping down, which eventually triggers most stocks to likewise open with space down. Investing thinks these are simply little missteps in the general photo of the long-lasting viewpoint.

Day traders have various requirements than financiers when looking for stocks. As discussed above, day traders are more focused on technical analysis than basic analysis. Day traders look for stocks with momentum and volatility.

Stock's can respond strongly to the business profits report and assistance. Years of earnings can be lost in a single session for missing out on agreement expert quotes and assistance figures. Financiers normally will choose whether to continue holding a position based on these outcomes where basic analysis plays a crucial part in the decision-making procedure.

The details are being provided without factor to consider the financial investment goals, danger tolerance, or monetary scenarios of any particular financier and may not be ideal for all financiers. Investing includes danger, consisting of the possible loss of principal.

The primary distinctions between day trading and investing are the activity levels and position holding times. Day traders focus on short-term trades consisted of in a single trading day using direct-access trading platforms.

PLATFORMS AND TOOLS FOR TRADING

A trading platform is a software application utilized for trading: opening, closing and handling market positions through a monetary intermediary such as an online broker. Online trading platforms are often provided by brokers either totally free or at a discount rate in exchange for keeping a financed account and/or making a defined variety of trades each month. The very best trading platforms use a mix of low charges and robust functions

Charges are another crucial factor to consider while selecting trading platforms. Traders who use scalping as a trading technique will gravitate towards platforms with low costs.

Traders utilize a range of various trading platforms depending upon their trading design and volume. Investopedia's Trading for Beginners Course offers an extensive intro to active trading if you're still brand-new to trading. You'll discover market terms, methods for determining patterns, and even construct your own trading system in over 5 hours of on-demand video, workouts, and interactive material.

There are two types of trading platforms: prop platforms and business platforms. Prop platforms, on the other hand, are tailored platforms established by big brokerages to match their particular requirements and trading design.

Some trading platforms might be agnostic to a particular intermediary or broker, while other trading platforms are just readily available when dealing with a specific intermediary or broker. As an outcome, financiers ought to likewise think about the credibility of the intermediary or broker prior to devoting to a particular trading platform to perform trades and handle their accounts.

Trading platforms might have particular requirements to certify for their usage. Day trading platforms might need that traders have at least $25,000 in equity in their accounts and be authorized for margin trading, while choices platforms might need the approval to trade numerous types of choices prior to being able to utilize the trading platform.

Trading platforms are software application tools utilized to perform and handle market positions.

Platforms vary from fundamental order entry screens for novice financiers to complex and advanced toolkits with live streaming quotes and charts for sophisticated traders.

When picking a trading platform, financiers and traders must take several factors to consider into account and balanced compromises.

1. Essentials of Trading Platform

A trading platform is the software application that makes it possible for traders and financiers to position trades and keep track of accounts through monetary intermediaries. Often, trading platforms will come bundled with other functions, such as real-time quotes, charting tools, news feeds, and even superior research study. Platforms might likewise be particularly customized to particular markets, such as stocks, futures, currencies, or alternatives markets.

1. Choosing a Platform

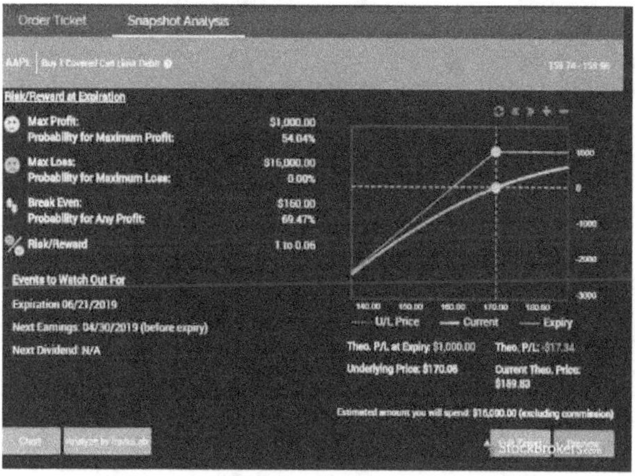

When choosing in between trading platforms, financiers and traders must think about both the costs included and includes offered. Day traders and other short-term traders might need functions like Level 2 quotes and market maker depth charts to help in decision-making, while alternatives traders might require tools that are particularly created to picture alternatives techniques.

2. Popular Trading Platforms

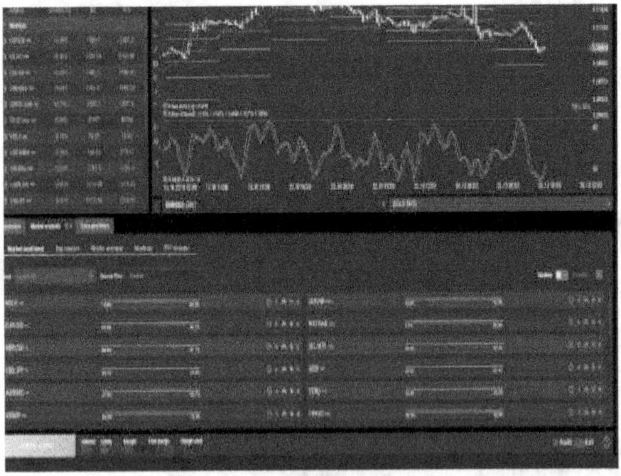

There are hundreds if not thousands of various trading platforms, consisting of these four popular choices:

Online trading needs getting the best details at the correct time to make educated choices, and if specific trading innovations assist you to enhance your returns when you purchase stocks online, they can quickly spend for themselves. If you have a portfolio with $100,000, a leading trading platform that assists you to produce an extra 1 per cent in returns is still an offer as long as your yearly commissions are within $1,000 of contending online stock brokers.

Beginner financiers are most likely going to value a simple, instinctive user interface that lets them see how their cash is carrying out and why that's essential. However, an active trader is visiting a lot more worth in a platform that accesses a range of up-to-the-second information feeds.

Numerous online brokers provide a selection of various platforms fine-tuned to various types of users, so you need to have plenty of alternatives for discovering the investing software application that matches you.

Interactive Brokers: Interactive Brokers is the most popular trading platform for experts with low charges and access to markets around the globe.

TradeStation: TradeStation is a popular trading platform for algorithmic traders that choose to perform trading methods utilizing automated scripts established with Easy Language.

TDAmeritrade: TDAmeritrade is a popular broker for both financiers and traders, particularly following its acquisition of ThinkorSwim and the advancement of the Trade Architect platforms.

Robinhood: Robinhood is a commission-free trading platform targeted at millennials. It began off as a mobile app and now has a web user interface. The platform earns money from numerous sources, from interest on money in its accounts to offering order circulation to big brokerages.

The most popular platform for numerous forex (forex) market individuals is MetaTrader, which is a trading platform that interfaces with various brokers. It's MQL scripting language has actually ended up being a popular tool for those seeking to automate trading in currencies.

Even if you can't measure much better returns, the long-lasting advantages of much better understanding your financial investments should not be marked down. If it implies you begin conserving and investing more, a platform with a user interface that assists you to feel more engaged and linked with your financial investments is certainly worth the expense.

1. TD Ameritrade

TD Ameritrade's thinkorswim platform offers innovative traders elite-level tools to prepare and carry out trades, while its standard web platform uses a range of standard research study and tools in one location for essential financiers. You can likewise utilize Social Signals to choose insights from Twitter, Portfolio Planner to handle your financial investments and paper money to check out theoretical techniques prior to putting your cash on the line.

2. Interactive Brokers

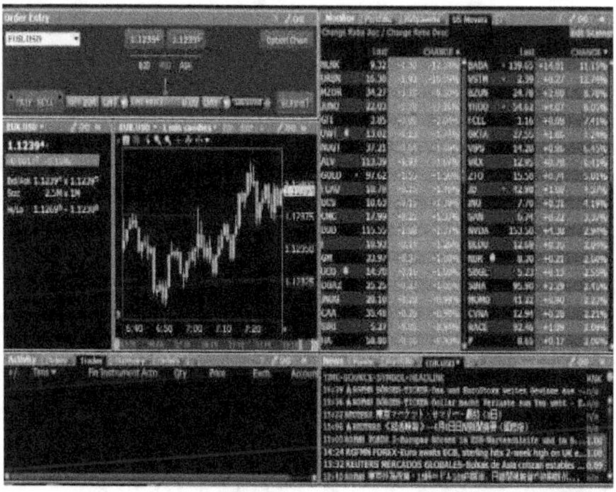

Interactive Brokers uses six various platforms that provide you access to trading by means of downloadable software application, its web platform or with your mobile phone. With these several gain access to alternatives, you'll get the PortfolioAnalyst tool and Probability Lab, which assists you check out choices trading without comprehending the complex mathematics included.

Charles Schwab lets you trade online at Schwab.com. However, it likewise has StreetSmart Edge, a personalized platform that you can adjust to your individual investing design. In addition to numerous information feeds and tools to assist you in choosing financial investments, the Gain/Loss Analyzer can assist you to comprehend the previous efficiency and use the lessons to future trades.

3. E-Trade

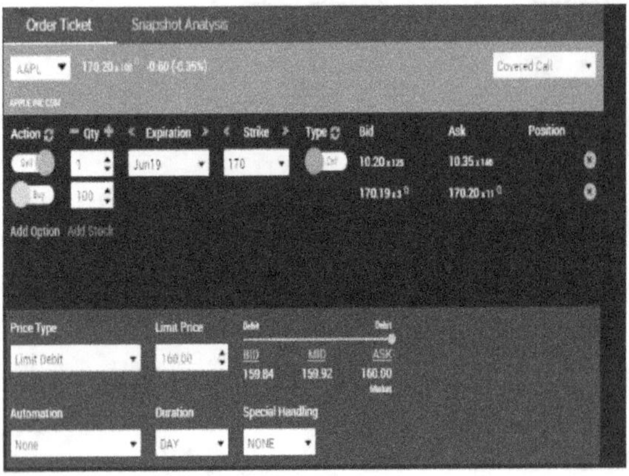

E-Trade's more intricate platform OptionsHouse provides knowledgeable traders with advanced charting and pro-level idea-generation tools to take advantage of their cash. Even on the fundamental web platform, you'll still get access to third-party research study, investing screeners and tools, and retirement preparation and instructional resources.

4. TradeStation

TradeStation uses its platform by means of desktop, web platform and on mobile, so you can utilize it from practically anywhere. You'll get access to TradeStation's blog site and market insights along with TradeStation Analytics, a desktop analysis platform that consists of real-time market scanning tools.

Forex trading (FX) is carried out online by means of an electronic trading platform. Naturally, lots of traders are curious as to what the finest trading platform software application is.

The trading software application market is greatly controlled by MetaQuotes Corp - the business behind MetaTrader 4 (MT4), which is the most popular software application utilized by traders in the retail Forex market. Whilst MetaTrader 4 is the dominant option for numerous expert traders, there are other choices which have actually established in the last few years.

5. MetaQuotes Platforms

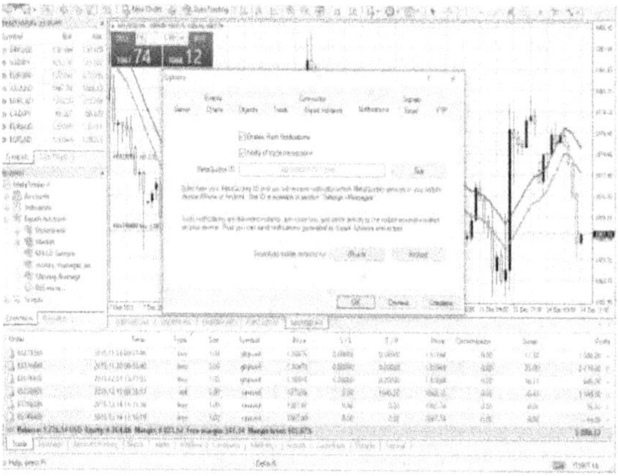

When it concerns trading FX online, a lot of brokers will provide you with different trading platforms, yet MetaTrader platforms are the most typical. This software application was established almost ten years earlier. There are two main options of the trading platform used by MetaQuotes Corp - MetaTrader 4 and MetaTrader 5.

6. Trading platforms and other stockbroker services

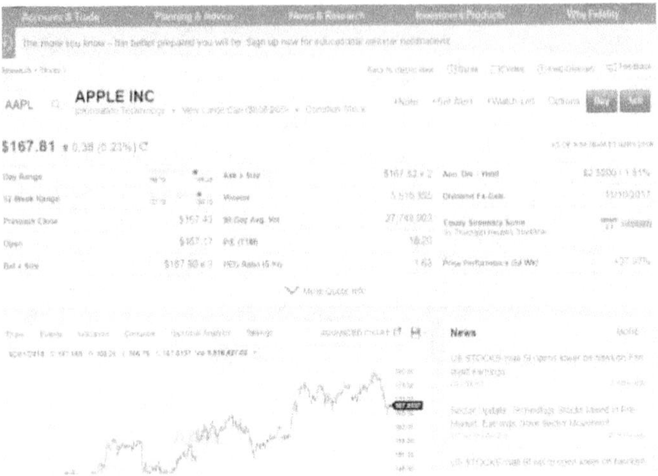

Apart from the trading platform, the primary service that such websites supply depends on the minute news and news feeders. Now you have at your disposal all the immediate news that the web offers, all the details bearing on your trading that you might want. Unless you are a stringent technical expert taking no notification of news or other occasions that might affect future rate motions, then you require continuously upgraded monetary and market news.

These are perhaps the tools that have actually progressed the most rapidly and to the best level. Even the initial, standard platforms that initially appeared in the late 1990s were advanced compared to the system we had prior to - utilizing the telephone to advise your broker. Now with the current advancements you can go into, change, or close a trade with simply a couple of mouse clicks, and it's practically (though not rather, naturally) sure-fire, with rates being shown immediately, various colours for trading, and so on.

7, Indicators and charts

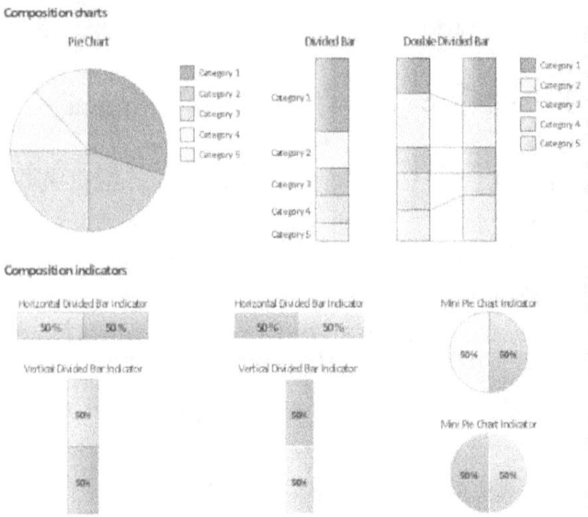

These have actually progressed beyond all acknowledgement. Many brokers, and numerous website not connected straight to any private broker, have charting services offered, which usually consist of a host of indications that are customisable to your requirements or those of your trading system.

Now charts are readily available on any stock, index, product, currency or bond traded on any monetary market, and most of the times they can return for ten years or more.

In seconds you can pack your own easy moving typical settings or any other sign or a mix of signs onto them.

A lot of stockbrokers have their own personalized training offered to their consumers. My own choice is for independent training from an effective and skilled trader, rather than a broker.

This is, without doubt, significant development and important property of the trader, both skilled and brand-new. There's a temptation to trade recklessly exactly due to the fact that it's not genuine cash. However, my recommendations are constantly to deal with is as genuine cash if you truly desire to discover and to have trustworthy outcomes, whether bad or great.

8. Trading robotics

At today time, they do not appear to be able to consider the truth that market value is affected by human beings, with all our psychological luggage. There's absolutely nothing to state they can't enhance and progress. In the meantime, if you're lured into purchasing one, testing it out completely with a demonstration account prior to running the risk of genuine cash with it.

These are the most recent tools to show up on the monetary trading scene. Originated in the forex market, they are starting to develop themselves as a traditional stock trade software application. In theory, you set your specifications, e.g. just how much of your capital to run the risk of on any one trade, stop loss levels, and load your selected indications or "professional consultants", and the robotic will open and close your trades for you, removing the human psychological aspect that so frequently causes losing trades.

.

OPTIONS TRADING BASICS

Alternatives trading isn't brand-new. The very first noted alternatives agreement made its launching on the Chicago Board Options Exchange in 1973.

The good aspect of a few of today's modern-day trading platforms, like thinkorswim ® from TD Ameritrade, is they make it possible to put an order for even a sophisticated technique with just one click. The choices market does the rest.

A choice is an agreement that enables (however does not need) a financier to purchase or offer a hidden instrument like a security, ETF or index at a particular cost over a specific amount of time. What is alternatives trading?

Calls and puts can be utilized in a myriad of methods to produce various prospective threats and benefits situations.

Complex techniques like calendars, butterflies and straddles lie outside the scope of this post, however, despite the alternative agreement or the inspiration for trading, the orders are sent to a brokerage company, and after that, the deals occur among the exchanges.

A put alternative represents the right to offer security at a pre-determined cost (the strike cost) for a specific amount of time. If they anticipate the cost of a stock to move lower or as a protective position, a financier may purchase a put. A put seller is obliged to purchase the stock at the strike cost through an expiration duration.

Financiers utilize choices for a range of various factors. A call choice is an agreement that provides the financier with the right to purchase a stock at a set rate for a specific duration of time.

If you want to operate the stock market or purchase a Market Traded Fund (ETF) or 2, you are more likely to grasp a variety of securities' essentialities. What precisely are alternatives, and what is choices trading?

Trading choices is a lot like trading stocks. However, there are necessary distinctions. Unlike stocks, choices are available in 2 types (calls and puts), and these choices are agreements (instead of shares) that provide the owner with the right to purchase or offer hidden security like a stock. Like stocks, nevertheless, alternatives are traded on exchanges, and specific financiers can position orders to offer and purchase through a brokerage company.

If it comes to trading in shares, there are a lot of opportunities if you haven't noticed by now.

What Are Options?

The other set element of a choice agreement is the expiration date. Due to the fact that of this particular, an alternative purchaser or holder has the danger of losing the whole premium paid to purchase that choice.

For both call and put alternatives, the more time left on the agreement, the greater the premiums are going to be.

On the contrary to call alternatives, with put choices, the greater the strike cost, the more intrinsic worth the put alternative has.

Why would a financier usage alternative? Well, purchasing choices is essentially banking on stocks to increase, down or to hedge a trading position in the market.

For call alternatives, the lower the strike rate, the more intrinsic worth the call choice has.

As a choice author, this will work in our favour. Once again, depending upon our goals, we will choose a suitable expiration date. You will see that there is a number of various strike costs noted for a particular expiration month, If the trader or financier desires to make the most of more time, an alternative agreement with the very same strike rate, however later on expiration month might be chosen.

Much like call choices, the rate at which you accept offer the stock is called the strike rate, and the premium is the charge you are spending for the put alternative.

If you're purchasing a call choice, it suggests you desire the stock (or other security) to increase in rate so that you can earn a profit off of your agreement by exercising your right to purchase those stocks (and typically instantly offer them to capitalize the revenue).

Long vs. Short Options

Unlike other securities like futures agreements, choices trading is generally a "long" - suggesting you are purchasing the choice with the hopes of the rate increasing (in which case you would purchase a call alternative). Even if you purchase a put alternative (right to offer the security), you are still purchasing a long choice.

The charge you are paying to purchase the call alternative is called the premium (it's basically the expense of purchasing the agreement which will permit you to ultimately purchase the stock or security). In this sense, the premium of the call alternative is sort of like a down-payment like you would put on a home or automobile. When acquiring a call alternatively, you concur with the seller on a strike rate and are provided with the alternative to purchase the security at an established rate (which does not alter up until the agreement ends).

Put Options

Alternatively, a put alternative is an agreement that provides the financier with the right to offer a particular quantity of shares (once again, normally 100 per agreement) of a specific security or product at a defined rate over a specific quantity of time. Much like call alternatives, a put alternative permits the trader the right (however not responsibility) to offer security by the agreement's expiration date.

Call alternatives are likewise much like insurance coverage - you are paying for an agreement that ends at a set time however enables you to acquire security (like a stock) at an established rate (which will not go up even if the rate of the stock on the market does). You will have to restore your choice (usually on a weekly, quarterly or month-to-month basis). For this factor, alternatives are constantly experiencing what's called time decay - suggesting their worth decomposes gradually.

The cost at which you accept purchase the hidden security through the choice is called the "strike cost," and the cost you spend on purchasing that choice agreement is called the "premium." When identifying the strike cost, you are wagering that the property (generally a stock) will increase or down in cost. The rate you are spending for that bet is the premium, which is a portion of the worth of that possession.

Alternatives part of a number of financial investment tools that make up the acquired market. With an understanding of their trading qualities, we can buy and offer choices on numerous various stocks, ETFs, currencies, products and futures.

Keep in mind that the strike rate is a set element of the alternatives agreement and each agreement trades separately from one another A put alternative chain is likewise built in the exact same way other than that the strike rates represent the rate at which a put choice purchaser or holder has the right to offer the hidden security. To the choice author or seller, this ends up being the cost at which they are needed to acquire the underlying ought to it be trading listed below the strike cost on expiration.

As an alternative author or seller, this is the cost at which a commitment to purchase or provide the hidden security has actually been developed. The strike cost is a set element of an alternative agreement When taking a look at the offered alternatives on a specific stock you will see under the strike column a series of various rates at which the choice trader has the capability to purchase the hidden security when it comes to a call alternative. It is necessary to bear in mind that to the individual who offers or composes the alternative call agreement, the strike cost shows the cost at which the commitment to provide the hidden security occur at needs to the hidden worth be trading above it by expiration.

As a suggestion, the expiration month for a call alternatives refers to the time in which the Call holder has the right to purchase the hidden security at the particular strike cost. Put alternative expiry times are observed in the same manner rather than, of course, this date applies to the period that a put alternative operator is allowed to deliver the secret protection at the actual expense of the attack.

There might be lots of various choices agreements trading on any one private underlying stock, each having its own set workout or strike rate. It is the cost at which the holder of the option has the freedom to buy (in the event of an alternative call) or offer (in the case of a placed alternative) the secret safe.

Put alternatives run in a comparable style to calls, other than you desire the security to drop in cost if you are purchasing a put alternative in order to earn a profit (or offer the put alternative if you believe the cost will increase)

Shorting a choice is offering that choice. However, the revenues of the sale are restricted to the premium of the alternative - and, the threat is limitless.

When purchasing or offering choices, the financier or trader deserves to work out that choice at any point up till the expiration date - so just offering an alternative or purchasing does not suggest you, in fact, need to exercise it at the buy/sell point. Due to the fact that of this system, choices are thought-about acquired securities - which indicates their rate is stemmed from something else (in this case, from the worth of properties like the marketplace, securities or other underlying instruments). For this factor, alternatives are frequently thought about less dangerous than stocks (if utilized properly).

When taking a look at a common choice chain, the quote and ask rate along with the last rate is shown for each agreement. Bear in mind that each of these contacts trades separately and are priced in a different way based upon the strike cost and expiration month.

There are two various sorts of alternatives - call and put choices - which provide the financier with the right (however not responsibility) to offer or purchase securities.

A choice is an agreement that enables (however does not need) a financier to purchase or offer a hidden instrument like a security, ETF and even index at an established cost over a specific time period. Purchasing and offering alternatives is done on the alternatives market, which trades agreements based upon securities. Purchasing an alternative that permits you to purchase shares at a later time is called a "call alternative," whereas purchasing a choice that permits you to offer shares at a later time is called a "put alternative."

Call Options

A call choice is an arrangement that grants the financier the opportunity to buy a certain number of stock (normally 100 stock per deal) in a particular asset or company at a defined cost for a specified period of time. A call choice would enable a trader to purchase a particular quantity of shares of either stock, bonds, or even other instruments like ETFs or indexes at a future time (by the expiration of the agreement)

Alternatives are not quite the same thing as securities, because they do not reflect ownership of a business. And, although futures utilize agreements similar to choices do, choices are a thought-about lower threat due to the truth that you can withdraw (or ignore) an alternatives agreement at any point. The rate of choice (it's premium) is hence a portion of the hidden property or security.

What Is Options Trading?

Well, you've thought it alternatives trading is just trading alternatives, and is generally made with securities on the stock or bond market (in addition to ETFs and so on).

Choices trading (specifically in the stock exchange) is impacted mainly by the rate of the hidden security, time up until the expiration of the alternative, and the volatility of the hidden security.

Another method to consider it is that call alternatives is typically bullish, while put choices are normally bearish.

Trading Call vs Put Options

Acquiring a call choice is basically wagering that the rate of the share of security (like stock or index) will increase throughout a fixed quantity of time. If you purchase a call alternative for Alphabet (GOOG) - Get Report at, state, $1,500 and are feeling bullish about the stock, you are anticipating that the share cost for Alphabet will increase.

When acquiring put choices, you are anticipating the cost of the hidden security to go down over time (so, you're bearish on the stock). In this case, due to the fact that you bought the put choice when the index was at $2,100 per share (presuming the strike rate was at or in cash), you would be able to offer the choice at that exact same cost (not the brand-new, lower cost).

When purchasing a call alternatively, the strike cost of an alternative for a stock, for instance, will be identified based upon the existing cost of that stock. If a share of an offered stock (like Amazon (AMZN) - Get Report) is $1,748, any strike cost (cost of the call choice) that is above that share rate is thought about to be "out of the cash." On the other hand, if the strike cost is under the existing share cost of the stock, it's thought about "in cash."

The premium of choice (its rate) is figured out by intrinsic worth plus its time worth (extrinsic worth).

For put alternatives (right to offer), the reverse is real - with strike rates listed below the existing share cost being thought about "out of the cash" and vice versa. And, what's more crucial - any "out of the cash" choices (whether call or put alternatives) are useless at expiration (so you truly wish to have an "in cash" alternative when trading on the stock exchange).

Historical vs Implied Volatility

If you are purchasing an option that is currently "in cash" (indicating the option will instantly remain in revenue), its premium will have an additional expense due to the fact that you can offer it right away for earnings. On the other hand, if you have an option that is "at the cash," the option amounts to the existing stock rate. And, as you might have thought, an option that is "out of the cash" is one that will not have extra worth since it is presently not in revenue.

For call choices, "in cash" agreements will be those whose hidden property's cost (stock, ETF, and so on) is above the strike rate. For put choices, the agreement will be "in cash" if the strike rate is listed below the present cost of the hidden property (stock, ETF, and so on).

When trading alternatives on the stock exchange, stocks with high volatility (ones whose share costs change a lot) are more pricey than those with low volatility (although due to the irregular nature of the stock exchange, even low volatility stocks can end up being high volatility ones ultimately).

The time worth, which is likewise called the extrinsic worth, is the worth of the option above the intrinsic worth (or, above the "in the cash" location).

High volatility of shares (like stocks) implies greater risk just like you might expect-while on the other side, and low volatility implies a lower hazard.

Volatility in asset investing explains how big the fluctuations in the market are for a product sold. The longer an option has prior to its expiration date, the more time it needs to in fact earn a profit, so its premium (cost) is going to be greater due to the fact that its time worth is greater. Alternatively, the less time an alternatives agreement has prior to it ends, the less its time worth will be (the less extra time worth will be contributed to the premium).

Historical volatility is a great step of volatility because it determines just how much a stock varied daily over a one year amount of time. In the other side, suggested volatility is a future-oriented asset (or security) volatility calculation centred on the markets over the option agreement's duration.

If an option (whether a put or call option) is going to be "out of the cash" by its expiration date, you can offer choices in order to gather a time premium.

In other terms, if an alternative requires a lot more time before it expires, the more time it spends will be included in the premium (cost)-so the less time it takes before expiry, the less time it takes would be included in the prime.

Options Trading Strategies

When trading alternatives, the agreements will generally take this kind:

When the stock rate boosts or stays quite consistent over the time of the option agreement, covered calls can make you cash. You might lose cash with this kind of trade if the stock rate falls too much (however can in fact still make cash if it just falls a little bit). By utilizing this method, you are really securing your financial investment from declines in share cost while providing yourself with the chance to make cash while the stock cost is flat.

Still, depending upon what platform you are trading on, the option trade will look really various.

The benefit of a strangle method is that there is less danger of loss because the premiums are more economical due to how the choices are "out of the cash" - indicating they're less expensive to purchase.

Covered Call

A covered call is an excellent option for you if you have long property financial investments (like stocks, for example). This technique is normally helpful for financiers who are somewhat bullish or just neutral on a stock.

Offering Iron Condors

For iron condors, the position of the trade is non-directional, which indicates the possession (like a stock) can either go up or down - so, there is revenue capacity for a relatively large variety. To utilize this kind of technique, offer a put and purchase another put at a lower strike cost (basically, a put spread), and integrate it by purchasing a call and offering a call at a greater strike rate (a call spread).

Options Trading Mistakes

You purchase an option for 100 shares of Oracle (ORCL) - Get Report for a strike rate of $40 per share which ends in 2 months, anticipating stock to go to $50 by that time. When the stock cost strikes $50 as you wager it would, your call option to purchase at $40 per share will be $10 "in cash" (the agreement is now worth $1,000, given that you have 100 shares of the stock) - considering that the distinction in between 40 and 50 is 10.

There are great deals of examples of alternatives trading that mostly depend upon which technique you are utilizing. As a fundamental concept of what a common call or put option would be, let's think about a trader purchasing a call and put option on Microsoft (MSFT) - Get Report.

If you purchased a long call option (keep in mind, a call option is an agreement that provides you with the right to purchase shares later on) for 100 shares of Microsoft stock at $110 per share for December 1, you would have the right to purchase 100 shares of that stock at $110 per share regardless of if the stock cost altered or not by December 1. You should anticipate Microsoft's pricing to increase for this long call option, thereby enabling you to reap the benefit because you have the opportunity to buy it at a less costly expense than its retail price. When you chose not to use the opportunity to purchase the stock, you will automatically forfeit the fee you charged for the choice because you are not allowed to buy the securities.

If you were purchasing a long put option for Microsoft, you would be wagering that the rate of Microsoft shares would reduce up till your agreement ends, so that, if you selected to exercise your right to offer those shares, you 'd be offering them at a greater cost than their market price.

Why Learning Options Trading Basics

And if alternative investing is that straightforward, then there will be plentiful investing options, that's where the logic ends sadly!

A put alternative helps you to sell anything at a defined rate. You are an oil manufacturer, and you understand that if you might offer your oil in May at the ensured cost of $80 per barrel you will make good earnings. You will have to offer the oil at $80 per barrel, and the broker will have to purchase it off you at that cost.

You presently lease your home, and your property owner provides you with the option to acquire the home for $200,000 in the next six months. Then you have to let the property manager pay and understand up $200,000 if you desire to purchase the home. The proprietor needs to offer to you as he contractually assured to do so.

What is an option? A choice offers you the ability to do it but not the obligation. Which means you don't have to do it if you don't want to.

An ideal way to figure out how the pro's deal is by actually watching them and copying them. A few of the very best men I have actually seen are at These men describe to you the fundamentals, reveal you how they earn money from alternatives trading and lets you copy them immediately if you wish to. Here you will find out not just the essentials in choices trading; however, likewise the tricks of how the experts generate income on a constant basis.

Which are all alternatives are? You make your cash by either offering them and letting the alternatives end or purchasing them and hoping the hidden possession you purchased the option on increases in worth.

The alternatives trading fundamentals can be summed up in 3 words: calls and puts.

If you do not wish to purchase then you do not need to do anything, and after six months the option will end, and your proprietor does not need to offer to you if he does not wish to. This would be an example of a call option an option which grants you the right to purchase something.

Due to the fact that these are the only two types of choices which are out there, the factor why I state this is. And if that was not easy enough, there are just two things you can do with either of them; purchase them or offer them.

Options Trading Made Easy

Enough understanding and experience on option trading fundamentals are what you require prior to embarking on this really dangerous type of financial investment. Workshops on option trading fundamentals can likewise be of terrific aid to guarantee that you can make excellent cash out of this financial investment.

When practised thoroughly, options trading is another financial investment lorry that can provide you with big returns. To begin finding out some option trading fundamentals, you should initially understand what alternatives are and how options trading works.

Little financiers are quickly drawn into trading choices due to the fact that it enables them to trade a really huge direct exposure with simply a little quantity of cash as capital. Professionals recommend that it is sensible to invest just in alternatives trading with threat capital.

The fundamental ideas of trading alternatives are the put and call choices, long and brief positions, intrinsic and time worth, and speculation and hedging. Alternatives have more danger than stocks since their preliminary worth decreases as the day passes up until it ends up being useless when it ends; therefore, the faster you offer them the much better. Keep in mind, likewise that those that are constantly closest to the cash trade have a lower threat and the supreme power of alternatives lies exclusively in their flexibility.

To launch your company with trading options, the most crucial aspect you can bear in mind is to pick to be very successful at this organization's place. You do need to select equity alternatives or an index with a lot of amount of trade and strong liquidity.

In addition to the previously mentioned simple options trading information, an options trader must also explore various option methods. Option rates can be utilized to check the danger and benefit profiles of various option methods that will assist you to comprehend the business of trading choices much better. For retail trading, just a basic option method is required.

Trading options, on the other hand, often offers tons of advantages relative to other kinds of financial activity. Similar to stock trading, trading options face a minimal threat with limitless earning capacity.

Another thing that you ought to understand about option trading essentials is where to trade option agreements. Many alternatives are traded through public exchange homes, and they can likewise be concurred in between 2 celebrations or what is understood as the over the counter market.

TRADING STRATEGIES FOR BEGINNERS

Online brokers on our list, consisting of Tradestation, TD Ameritrade, and Interactive Brokers, have innovative or expert variations of their platforms that include real-time streaming quotes, advanced charting tools, and the capability to get in and customize intricate orders in fast succession.

When traders take it seriously and do their research study, day trading is just rewarding.

Day trading is a task, not a pastime or passing trend of activity. Treat it as such-- be persistent, focused, goal, and separate feelings.

Here we supply some standard pointers and knowledge to end up being an effective day trader.

Let's have a look at some basic day trading concepts and after that, proceed to choose when to offer and purchase, typical day trading techniques, standard charts and patterns, and how to restrict losses.

Day trading is the act of purchasing and offering a monetary instrument within the very same day or even numerous times over the course of a day. What's more, not all brokers are fit for the high volume of trades made by day traders. You can inspect out our list of the finest brokers for day trading to see which brokers best accommodate those who would like to day trade.

1. Understanding Is Power

In addition to the understanding of standard trading treatments, day traders require to keep up on the most current stock market news and occasions that impact stocks-- the Fed's interest rate strategies, the financial outlook, and so on. Make a dream list of stocks you 'd like to trade and keep yourself notified about the chosen business and basic markets.

2. Reserve Funds

Lots of effective day traders run the risk of less than 1% to 2% of their account per trade. If you have a $40,000 trading account and are ready to run the risk of 0.5% of your capital on each trade, your optimum loss per trade is $200 (0.005 x $40,000).

3. Reserve Time, Too

Day trading needs your time. That's why it's called day trading. You'll require to offer up many of your days.

4. Start Small

As a newbie, concentrate on an optimum of one to 2 stocks throughout a session. Tracking and discovering changes is simpler, with simply a couple of stocks.

Just recently, it has actually ended up being progressively typical to be able to trade fractional shares, so you can define particular, smaller sized dollar quantities you want to invest. That indicates if Apple shares are trading at $250 and you just wish to purchase $50 worth, numerous brokers will now let you acquire one-fifth of a share.

5. Prevent Penny Stocks

You're most likely looking for offers and low costs, however, remain away from cent stocks. Numerous stocks trading under $5 a share ended up being delisted from significant stock exchanges and are just tradable non-prescription (OTC).

What Makes Day Trading Difficult?

Understand that you're going up versus experts whose professions revolve around trading. These individuals have access to the very best innovation and connections in the market, so even if they stop working, they're established to be successful in the end. It indicates more earnings for them if you leap on the bandwagon.

As a private financier, you might be susceptible to mental and psychological predispositions. Expert traders are typically able to cut these out of their trading methods; however, when it's your own capital included, it tends to be a various story.

Day trading takes a great deal of practice and knowledge, and there are numerous elements that can make the procedure difficult.

Uncle Sam will likewise desire a cut of your earnings, no matter how slim. Keep in mind that you'll need to pay taxes on any short-term gains or any financial investments you hold for one year or less at the limited rate. The one caution is that your losses will balance out any gains.

When to Buy, choosing What and

Day traders attempt to earn money by making use of minute rate motions in specific possessions (stocks, choices, futures, and currencies), normally leveraging large quantities of capital to do so. In choosing what to concentrate on in a stock, state a normal day trader tries to find three things:

Liquidity: Liquidity enables you to leave stock and go into at a great cost. Tight spreads or the distinction in between the quote and ask the cost of a stock, and low slippage or the distinction in between the anticipated rate of a trade and the real rate.

Volatility: Volatility is merely a procedure of the anticipated day-to-day rate variety the variety in which a day trader runs. More volatility suggests higher revenue or loss.

Trading volume: This is a step of the number of times a stock is purchased and offered in an offered period most typically referred to as the typical day-to-day trading volume. A high degree of the volume shows a great deal of interest in a stock. A boost in a stock's volume is frequently a precursor of a cost dive, either up or down.

When you understand what sort of stocks (or other properties) you're trying to find, you require to discover how to recognize entry points that are, at what exact minute you're going to invest. Tools that can assist you to do this consist of:

ECN/Level 2 quotes: ECNs, or electronic interaction networks, are computer-based systems that show the very best readily available quote and ask quotes from several market individuals and after that immediately match and carry out orders. Level 2 is a subscription-based service that offers real-time access to the Nasdaq order book made up of estimate from market makers signing up every Nasdaq-listed and OTC Bulletin Board security. Together, they can offer you a sense of orders being carried out in genuine time.

Write and specify down the conditions under which you'll get in a position. "Buy throughout uptrend" isn't particular enough. Something like this is far more likewise testable and particular: "Buy when rating breaks above the upper trendline of a triangle pattern, where the triangle was preceded by an uptrend (a minimum of one greater swing high and greater swing low prior to the triangle formed) on the two-minute chart in the very first 2 hours of the trading day."

When you have a particular set of entry guidelines, scan through more charts to see if those conditions are created every day (presuming you wish to day trade every day) and typically produce a cost relocation in the expected instructions. You have a prospective entry point for a method if so. You'll then require to examine how to leave, or offer, those trades.

When to Sell, choosing

There are several methods to leave a winning position, consisting of tracking stops and earnings targets. Earnings targets are the most typical exit technique, taking a revenue at a pre-determined level. Some typical rate target techniques are:

Much like your entry point, specify precisely how you will leave your trades prior to entering them. The exit requirements need to specify sufficient to be testable and repeatable.

Scalping

Scalping is among the most popular methods. It includes offering nearly instantly after a trade ends up being lucrative. The cost target is whatever figure that equates into "you've generated income on this offer."

FadingFading includes shorting stocks after fast relocations up. Here, the cost target is when purchasers start stepping in once again.

Daily Pivots

This technique includes making money from a stock's day-to-day volatility. This is done by trying to purchase the low of the day and cost the high of the day. Here, the rate target is just at the next indication of a turnaround.

Momentum

The other type will fade the rate rise. Here, the rate target is when volume starts to reduce.

You'll desire to leave a possession when there is reduced interest in the stock as suggested by the Level 2/ECN and volume. The earnings target ought to likewise permit more earnings to be made on winning trades than is lost on losing trades. Your target needs to be more than $0.05 away if your stop-loss is $0.05 away from your entry rate.

Day Trading Charts And Patterns

To assist identify the appropriate minute to purchase a stock (or whatever property you're trading), numerous traders make use of:

- ✓ Candlestick patterns, consisting of swallowing up candle lights and dojis
- ✓ Technical analysis, consisting of pattern lines and triangles
- ✓ Volume-- reducing or increasing

There are numerous candlestick setups a day trader can search for to discover an entry point. The Doji turnaround pattern (highlighted in yellow in the chart listed below) is one of the most dependable ones if utilized effectively

How To Limit Losses When Day Trading

A physical stop-loss order positioned at a particular cost level that matches your danger tolerance. Basically, this is the most cash you can stand to lose.

A psychological stop-loss set at the point where your entry requirements are broken. This indicates if the trade makes an unanticipated turn, you'll right away leave your position.

You choose to leave your trades, and the exit requirements need to be particular adequate to be repeatable and testable. It's crucial to set an optimal loss per day you can pay for to stand up to-- both economically and psychologically. Take the rest of the day off. Whenever you strike this point.

Specify precisely how you'll manage the danger on the trades. When it comes to a triangle pattern, for example, a stop loss can be positioned $0.02 listed below a current swing low if purchasing a breakout, or $0.02 listed below the pattern. (The $0.02 is approximate; the point is just to be particular.).

Keep in mind that if trading on margin-- which suggests you're obtaining your financial investment funds from a brokerage company (and bear in mind that margin requirements for day trading are high) you're far more susceptible to sharp rate motions. Margin assists to enhance the trading results not simply of revenues, however of losses also if trade breaks you. Utilizing stop losses is vital when day trading on margin.

You can examine whether the prospective method fits within your threat limitation as soon as you've specified how you go into trades and where you'll position a stop loss. You require to modify the technique in some method to decrease the threat if the technique exposes you too much danger.

For long positions, a stop loss can be positioned listed below a current low, or for brief positions, above a current high. If a stock rate is moving about $0.05 a minute, then you might put a stop loss $0.15 away from your entry to provide the rate with some area to vary prior to it moves in your expected instructions.

One method is to set 2 stop losses.

Now that you understand a few of the ins and outs of day trading let's take a short take a look at a few of the essential methods brand-new day traders can utilize.

By hand go through historical charts to discover your entries, keeping in mind whether your stop loss or target would have been struck. Paper trade in this method for at least 50 to 100 trades, keeping in mind whether the technique was successful and if it satisfies your expectations. If it's lucrative over the course of 2 months or more in a simulated environment, continue with day trading the method with genuine capital.

Stay with your strategy and your borders.

Basic Day Trading Strategies

You will use a set of methods to assist you in your earnings task when you have learned some of the techniques, developed your own individual trading designs and defined what your target is.

Here are some common techniques. You can use. Some of these have actually been discussed above, and they are worth going into once again:

It will likewise describe some local distinctions to be knowledgeable about, in addition to pointing you in the instructions of some helpful resources. Eventually, however, you'll require to discover a day trading method that matches your particular trading design and requirements.

Following the pattern: Anyone who follows the pattern will purchase when costs are increasing or brief sell when they drop. This is done on the presumption that rates that have actually been increasing or falling progressively will continue to do so.

Contrarian investing: This method presumes the increase in costs will drop and reverse. The contrarian buys throughout the fall or short-sells throughout the increase, with the express expectation that the pattern will alter.

Scalping: This is a design where a speculator makes use of little rate spaces produced by the bid-ask spread. This strategy generally includes going into and leaving a position rapidly-- within minutes and even seconds.

Trading on the news: Investors utilizing this technique will purchase when great news is revealed or brief sell when there's bad news. This can cause higher volatility, which can result in greater losses or earnings.

Day trading is challenging to master. Numerous of those who attempt it stops working; however, the standards and methods explained above can assist you in developing a rewarding technique.

Day trading methods are necessary when you want to capitalise on regular, little cost motions. A constant, reliable technique depends on extensive technical analysis, using indications, patterns and charts to anticipate future rate motions. This page will offer you an extensive break down of beginners trading techniques, working all the method as much as innovative, even asset-specific and automatic techniques.

Guarantee your option of broker fits technique based day trading. You will desire things like;

Prior to you get slowed down in a complicated world of extremely technical indications, concentrate on the essentials of a basic day trading technique. Lots of making the error of believing you require an extremely made complex method to be successful intraday, however frequently the more uncomplicated, the more efficient.

The Basics.

Include the indispensable components listed below into your method.

Finance-- Before you begin, take a seat and choose just how much you're prepared to run the risk of. Remember, most effective traders will not put more than 2% of their capital on the line per trade. When the wins begin rolling in, you have to prepare yourself for some losses if you desire to be around.

If you just assign an hour or two a day to trading, Time management-- Don't anticipate to make a fortune. You require to continuously keep an eye on the marketplaces and watch for trade chances.

Start little-- Whilst you're discovering your feet, stay with an optimum of 3 stocks throughout a single day. It's much better to get actually proficient at a couple of than to be typical and making no cash on loads.

Education-- Understanding market complexities isn't enough, and you likewise require to remain notified. Ensure you keep up to date with market news and any occasions that will affect your possession, such as a shift in financial policy. You can discover a wealth of online monetary and service resources that will keep you in understanding.

When you're five coffees in, and you've been gazing at the screen for hours, consistency-- It's more difficult than it looks to keep feelings at bay. You require to let mathematics, reasoning and your technique guide you, not nerves, worry, or greed.

Timing-- The market will get unstable when it opens every day, and while skilled day traders might have the ability to check out the patterns and earnings, you need to bide your time. Hold back for the very first 15 minutes, and you've still got hours ahead.

Demonstration Account-- An essential tool for any novice, however likewise the very best location to backtest or explore brand-new, or fine-tuned, techniques for innovative traders. Lots of demonstration accounts are limitless, so not time-limited.

Elements Every Strategy Needs.

Whether you're after automatic day trading techniques, or newbie and innovative methods, you'll require to take into consideration three important parts; liquidity, volume and volatility. Selecting the ideal stock is essential if you're to make cash on small cost motions. These three components will assist you in making that choice.

- ✓ Exceptional trade execution speed,
- ✓ If possible), cost action information
- ✓ Capability to trade directly from charts.
- ✓ Trade automation.
- ✓ Stop losses and take revenue orders.

Go to the broker's page to guarantee you have the best trading partner in your broker.

Liquidity-- This allows you to quickly get in and leave trades at a steady and appealing cost. Liquid product techniques, for instance, will concentrate on gold, petroleum and gas.

Volatility-- This informs you your prospective earnings variety. The higher the volatility, the higher revenue or loss you might make. The cryptocurrency market is one such example popular for high volatility.

Volume-- This measurement will inform you how lots of times the stock/asset has actually been traded within a set duration of time. A boost in volume is often an indication a rate dive either up or down, is quickly approaching.

1. Breakout.

Breakout methods centre around when the cost clears a defined level on your chart, with increased volume. The breakout trader participates in a long position after the property or security breaks above resistance. You get in a brief position once the stock breaks listed below assistance.

You require to discover the best instrument to trade. When doing this, keep in mind the possession's assistance and resistance levels. The more regularly the cost has actually struck these points, the more verified and crucial they end up being.

After a possession or security trades beyond the defined cost barrier, volatility generally increases, and costs will typically trend in the instructions of the breakout.

Utilize the possession's current efficiency to develop a sensible cost target. If the typical rate swing has actually been 3 points over the last numerous rate swings, this would be a reasonable target..

The aspect is nice and uncomplicated. Prices set to close and higher rates of resistance need a bearish role. Tariffs scheduled to close and reported below a degree of support need a bullish stance.

2. Scalping back.

One of the most common scalping methods is. It's especially popular in the forex market, and it looks to capitalise on minute cost modifications. You require a high trading possibility to even out the low threat vs benefit ratio.

Watch for unstable instruments, appealing liquidity and be hot on timing. You can't wait on the marketplace, and you require to close losing trades as quickly as possible.
Popular scalping trading method.

3. Momentum.

Popular among trading techniques for beginners, this technique focuses on acting upon news sources and determining significant trending relocations with the assistance of high volume. There is constantly a minimum of one stock that moves 20-30% every day, so there's sufficient chance. You just keep your position up until you see indications of turnaround and after that go out.

If utilized properly, this technique is efficient and basic. You need to guarantee you're conscious of upcoming news and incomes statements. Simply a couple of seconds on each trade will make all the distinction to your end of daily earnings. Momentum day trading methods on the chart.

You can fade the rate drop. Round the goal rate, this way is as soon as volume starts to decrease.

4. Turnaround.

Fiercely discussed and possibly hazardous when utilized by beginners, reverse trading is utilized all over the world. It's likewise called pattern trading, drawback trending and a mean reversion method.

The 'everyday pivot' method is thought about a distinct case of reverse trading, as it centres on purchasing and offering the day-to-day low and high pullbacks/reverse Turnaround day trading methods on a chart.

This method defies fundamental reasoning as you intend to trade versus the pattern. You require to be able to properly determine possible pullbacks, plus anticipate their strength. To do this efficiently, you require a thorough market understanding and experience.

5. Utilizing Pivot Points.

A day trading pivot point technique can be great for acting and recognizing crucial assistance and/or resistance levels. This is especially useful in the forex sector. In addition, it can be utilized by range-bound traders to determine points of entry, while pattern and breakout traders can utilize pivot indicate find crucial levels that require to break for a relocate to count as a breakout. Determining Pivot Points.

A pivot point is specified as a point of rotation. You utilize the costs of the previous day's low and high, plus the closing rate of security to computing the pivot point.

Keep in mind that if you determine a pivot point utilizing cost info from a reasonably brief time frame, precision is frequently decreased.

How do you compute a pivot point?

One popular method is to set up two stop-losses. You put a physical stop-loss order at a particular cost level. If the trade makes an unexpected turn, you'll make a speedy exit.

Cryptocurrency Trading Strategies.

The unforeseeable and interesting cryptocurrency market uses lots of chances for the turned-on day trader. You do not require to comprehend the complex technical makeup of bitcoin or ethereum, nor do you require to hold a long-lasting view on their practicality. Merely utilize uncomplicated techniques to benefit from this unpredictable market.

The stop-loss manages your threat for you. In a brief position, you can position a stop-loss above a current high, for long positions you can put it listed below a current low. You can likewise make it dependant on volatility.

It's likewise worth keeping in mind, and this is among the systems & techniques that can be used to indexes too. It can assist form an efficient S&P day trading method.

Forex techniques are dangerous by nature as you require to collect your earnings in a brief area of time. You can use any of the methods above to the forex market, or you can see our forex page for in-depth method examples.

- ✓ First Resistance (R1) = (2 * P)-- Low.
- ✓ First Support (S1) = (2 * P)-- High.

The 2nd level of assistance and resistance is then determined as follows.

- ✓ Second Resistance (R2) = P + (R1-S1).
- ✓ Second Support (S2) = P-- (R1- S1).
- ✓ Application.

When used to the FX market, for instance, you will discover the trading variety for the session typically occurs in between the very first assistance and the pivot point and resistance levels. Since a high number of traders play this variety, this is Limit Your Losses.

Requirements for which are generally high for day traders. When you trade on margin, you are progressively susceptible to sharp rate motions.

Central Pivot Point (P) = (Low + high + Close)

You can then determine assistance and resistance levels utilizing the pivot point. To do that you will require to utilize the following solutions.

A stock rate relocations by £ 0.05 a minute, so you put a stop-loss £ 0.15 away from your entry order, enabling it to swing (ideally in the anticipated instructions).

To discover particular cryptocurrency methods,

Day trading methods for stocks count on much of the exact same concepts laid out throughout this page, and you can utilize much of the techniques described above. However, the methodology you should use for the stock exchange is described below.

Moving Average Convergence You would require three standard moving lines: you may also find that various nations have specific tax loopholes.

If you're based in the West however desire to use your regular day trading techniques in the Philippines, you require to do your research.

For CFD particular day trading suggestions and techniques, see our CFD page.

Laws are another element to think about. Indian techniques might be custom-made to fit within particular guidelines, such as high minimum equity balances in margin accounts. Get online and inspect odd guidelines will not affect your method prior to you put your difficult made cash on the line.

Now you should make a single trade to figure out how many trades you should manage, divide those 275 by 0.20.

You will pick up as many as 1,375 shares to a place level. That is the optimal place you would need to continue with your 1 per cent cap on the hazard.

Regional Differences

Various markets include various chances and obstacles to conquer. When you use them in Australia, day trading techniques for the Indian market might not be as efficient. Some nations might be wondering about the news, so the market might not respond in the exact same method as you 'd anticipate them to back house.

Position size

It will, likewise allow you to choose the best position size. Position size is the number of shares taken on a single trade.

In addition, you will discover they are tailored towards traders of all experience levels. You can discover for beginners PDFs and advanced PDFs. You can even discover country-specific choices, such as day trading suggestions and techniques for India PDFs.

Danger Management

Techniques that work take danger into account. You'll lose more than you can be and pay for out of the video game prior to you understand it if you do not handle the threat. This is why you must constantly use a stop-loss.

PDFs

PDFs are typically a wonderful location to go if you desire an in-depth list of the finest day trading methods. Their very first advantage is that they are simple to follow. You can have them open as you attempt to follow the guidelines by yourself candlestick charts.

CFDs are worried about the distinction in between where a trade is gotten in and exit. Current years have actually seen their appeal rise. This is since you can benefit when the underlying possession relocations in relation to the position taken, without ever needing to own the hidden possession.

Smart traders do not typically run the risk of more than 1% of their account balance on a single trade. If you have £ 27,500 in your account, you can run the risk of up to £ 275 per trade.

See our spread wagering page if you would like to see some of the finest day trading methods exposed.

You'll open a position when the typical moving line crosses in one instruction, and you'll close the position when it crosses back the opposite method.

You can discover a day trading techniques utilizing rate action patterns PDF download with a fast google.

Discovering a particular product or forex PDFs is reasonably simple.

Spread Betting Strategies

Spread wagering permits you to hypothesize on a substantial variety of worldwide markets without ever, in fact, owning the property. Plus, techniques are fairly uncomplicated.

For additional information on stocks techniques, see our Shares and stocks page.

- ✓ One set at 60 durations-- This is your sluggish moving average
- ✓ One set at 20 durations-- This is your quick-moving average
- ✓ One set at 100 durations-- This is your pattern sign

When the quick-moving typical crosses up and over the sluggish moving average, this is one of the moving averages methods that produce a buy signal. When the quick-moving typical crosses listed below the sluggish moving average, a sell signal is produced just.

Blog sites

In some cases, online blog sites are the location to go if you're looking for the finest day trading methods that work. Frequently complimentary, you can find out within day methods and more from knowledgeable traders. Blog sites are frequently an excellent source of motivation.

How can you develop there's absolutely a pattern? If the cost bar remains above or listed below the 100-period line, you understand the pattern is on.

CFD Strategies

Establishing a reliable day trading method can be made complex. Decide for an instrument such as a CFD and your task might be rather much easier.

Online forums

Plus, you typically discover day trading techniques so simple anybody can utilize. Due to the restricted area, you typically just get the essentials of day trading techniques.

What kind of tax will you need to pay? Will you need to pay it abroad and/or locally? Limited tax significant differences might make a considerable effect on your end of daily earnings.

Knowing Methods

Some will discover day trading methods videos most beneficial. This is why a number of brokers now use various types of day trading methods in easy-to-follow training videos.

Check there is enough volume in the stock/asset to take in the position size you utilize. In addition, remember that if you take a position size too huge for the marketplace, you might come across slippage on your entry and stop-loss.

The cost might appear like it's relocating the instructions you hoped. However, it might reverse at any time. A stop-loss will manage that threat. If the property or security does not come through, you'll leave the trade and just sustain a very little loss.

THE BEHAVIOUR OF A TRADER

Both take a 3rd individual viewpoint. They take a look at the behaviour of others and attempt to understand them.

If I am sincere, up until then, I had actually mostly endured as a trader.-- Though that was not how I saw it at the time.

We go with the concepts and approaches of others when we find out to trade. Someplace along the line, we should establish a method of working which fits ourselves.

Impulsively closing a brief

A spontaneous trading choice damaged my possibilities of earning a profit on this trade.

I need to've borne in mind that Stochastic crossing 50 is an indication that a pattern will be kept. I didn't have verification that the pattern was reversing. I simply didn't wish to lose any more cash, so my psychological self chose it was time to go out!:

At the start, the trader fell for the lure of making simple cash. When he lastly got out, he felt a sense of relief which is rather paradoxical because he had actually simply lost 70 per cent of his cash. Preparation, where to get out prior to putting on the trade, is a way of imposing psychological discipline."

Then you're continuously on the back foot if you do not have discipline. You're constantly believing, "now is it time to go out?", "how about now?"

While this is occurring the marketplace is moving. Perhaps in your instructions. Perhaps versus you.

All the while, your feelings are pulling you one method and after that the other. "I simply require to make another $100 on this trade, and after that, I'll go out."

You must be investing your energy and time taking a look at another market, preparing your next trade, rather of stressing over the present one. It's a huge diversion.

- ✓ How to enhance your discipline
- ✓ Discipline is the bridge between objectives and achievement."
- ✓ Discipline is a challenging monster to tame. I'm not going to sugar coat it.
- ✓ Here are some things you can do to enhance your trading discipline:
- ✓ Strategy your trades

Prior to you put any cash on the line choose what requires to occur in the market for you to go into a position.

In preparing you must get ready for two possibilities: the cost increasing and the rate decreasing.

In both scenarios, you require to understand where the rate requires to go to verify you're incorrect, and where you're going to get out if you're.

You're currently ahead of 90% of traders if you begin your profession off by believing about what occurs when you're incorrect.

As you may understand, these patterns tend to breakout ultimately. You do not understand which method it'll go. If the cost breaks out on the benefit, then have a buy order all set.

Where does the cost required to go to validate that you're incorrect? All the method to the bottom of the triangle? You have to make that choice.

I'm not stating you can't utilize other individuals' concepts trading. Simply that you need to comprehend why other individuals trade by doing this and decide your own. Otherwise, you will not have the ability to adhere to it.

- ✓ Trade your strategy
- ✓ This is the hardest part.

You made a strategy, now adhere to it.

You made logical choices with a clear head when your judgment wasn't clouded by the red in your PnL.

Trading your strategy is the most crucial thing, due to the fact that preparation is a waste without it.

It's well and great for me to inform you this. However, it's much easier stated than done, so I'll offer you some methods to assist you to adhere to your strategy:

Produce a trading list

Jot down all the requirements you require to be real for you to get in a position, and tick them off as they take place.

Do not go into a trade-up until all of the requirements have actually been marked off.

2. Start little

"One male informed another that he might not sleep on account of his position in the market; his pal sensibly and laconically responded: "Sell down to a sleeping point. ".

This suggests little positions, little scope, and little earnings targets.

Even if you begin little, does not indicate you can't increase your size and scope gradually.

The larger the position, the higher your psychological accessory. The more you have to lose, the more you're going to stress about it, and the more it's going to cloud your judgment.

Trading is not a get-rich-quick plan. It takes time and effort to develop up the abilities needed to regularly make huge cash.

Up until you've acquired experience, you require to begin little.

Focus on one property, due to the fact that you're a brand-new trader. That'll come with time and experience.

Following several possessions is going to lead you to get puzzled by all the various signals. As soon as you have those, and you're regularly making cash then feel totally free to include another property.

As a brand-new trader, you require to develop self-confidence in your capability by making some winning trades. Simply concentrate on remaining in the black and including little wins to your equity. Then you can think about increasing your position size as soon as you're regularly making little wins.

Once again, the focus here is to decrease your psychological accessory to your trades. If you're hanging all your hopes off one huge trade, then naturally you're going to consider it continuously, stress over it, and second-guess yourself..

Behavioural Finance takes a look at the marketplaces and financier behaviour to understand what is taking place.

The more you understand and can understand how you work as a trader, and the more you can begin to take control of how you work as a trader, and the more you can establish and hone your edge.

It was not rather a light switch going on, however rather the start of a brand-new stage which grew out of control in the years ahead. The years after the training were, without a doubt, the very best of my profession.

Utilizing the metaphor of the music charts, my profession till then had actually seen me produce a couple of hits and even a primary. However, I might not state hand on heart, 'I was a truly excellent trader'.

Establishing your 'Behavioural Trading' Capability.

'Behavioural Trading' assists individuals to craft a method of trading which fits themselves.

Behavioural Trading has to do with understanding yourself as a trader or financier. Ending up being mindful of yourself, of who you are, how you work, what requires you have, and exercising how you are going to satisfy them.

I worked as a trader for over 20 years, and for the previous ten years have actually been training traders from throughout the buy-side and the sell-side of markets. The concept that you can assist somebody who does not have the discipline to all of a sudden end up being disciplined is rubbish, and however, similarly, it does not indicate they can not end up being an effective trader.

Do you need to know the single behaviour that separates terrific traders from great traders? In this post, we'll go over the characters in addition to methods you can utilize to establish the characteristic in yourself.

The quality we're going to speak about is one that permits the very best traders to keep earning money year-after-year. It assists traders to make constant returns and keep the cash that they make in the market. It can not be undervalued.

You can have all the trading understanding and ability that you desire, however without this characteristic, and you'll be irregular which will restrict your capacity as a trader. You put a lot of effort into making cash in your very first year and then lost the big bulk of it.

Huge swings in returns like this recommend that something is missing your method.

- ✓ What's missing out on?
- ✓ What's the quality?
- ✓ Discipline.

The dictionary meaning of "discipline" is:

" the practice of training individuals to follow guidelines or a code of behaviour, utilizing penalty to fix disobedience."

In some method losing cash on bad trades might be seen as a penalty. This is a side result of not following your trading guidelines. However, it's not the wanted result.

In some cases, you may even MAKE cash by not following your trading guidelines, which can be a really complicated scenario.

I 'd like to restrict the meaning as utilized here to, "the practice of training individuals to comply with guidelines or a code of behaviour". That brings it more into the world of self-discipline.

It might be a surprise to you that the characteristic is not technical. It's not related to a traders capability to comprehend essential aspects or examine technical patterns on a chart.

There are plenty of examples of traders who made huge losses from an absence of discipline. If you've checked out Jack D. Schwager's, The Market Wizards, you'll understand that virtually every trader he spoke with had a story to share about how they blew up this account or almost cleaned out due to the fact that of one spontaneous trade.

"The desire for continuous action regardless of underlying conditions is accountable for lots of losses in Wall Street."

Jesse Livermore, the topic of "Reminiscences of a Stock Operator", was a stock exchange trader in the early 1900s. He notoriously acquired and lost numerous fortunes in the market, especially after shorting the 1907 and 1929 stock exchange crashes. He deserved $3 million and $100 million after each, respectively, and continued to lose most of his wealth on both events.

To put this in viewpoint, $100 million deserves about $1.5 $13 billion today, depending upon the index utilized. No matter the index, that's a helluva great deal of cash to lose and make by any basic!

Absence of discipline triggered Livermore to lose all that cash. Plainly he was a proficient trader, as he developed up a big fortune for himself on numerous events. The substantial psychological swings of making hundreds of millions of dollars, when others are losing their t-shirts.

Livermore dedicated suicide in 1940 and the note he left his other half-read,

Can't assist it. This is the only method out. I am genuinely sorry. However, this is the only method out for me.

The psychological pressure was excessive for him. Having more discipline may not have just secured Livermore's fortune; it may likewise have actually conserved his life.

"The market is a gadget for moving cash from the impatient to the client."

Throughout his life, Warren Buffet has actually accumulated a fortune of $87.5 billion (since February 2018), making him the 3rd wealthiest individual worldwide.

Yes, he's a financier, and what Buffet does is really various to what you wish to do, trade. The buffet is the reverse of the stereotyped trader, and his preferred holding duration is permanent.

The buffet is revealed excellent discipline. He understands what his strengths are, and he utilizes them. He understands what he's searching for in an organisation, has the discipline not to purchase anything that he hasn't thoroughly investigated, and does not purchase into a business or market he does not comprehend.

Buffet prepares his financial investments and buys his strategies.

Without discipline, Buffet may still be running pinball devices out of barber stores in Omaha or reselling and gathering lost golf balls from the Elmwood Park golf course.

I'm not stating you require to have a long-lasting view, or stop day trading to hold cryptos longer. Do not let yourself wander off from the course that you plainly laid out prior to you got in the market.

The economy will go up and down, and you'll lose cash for other places. During this time, you have to hold to your plan because you believed it though with a straight mind, without any market-triggered feelings.

Why Is It Important?

"Who appreciates discipline?! I just want to produce whatever profit I can!" You have to appreciate discipline as it has two tremendous effects on your company. Absence of discipline will trigger you to:

Go into bad, spontaneous trades, when your subjective, psychological self is managing your actions, not your goal, logical self. You may lose cash, and you may not. However, you're putting excessive to luck

Destroy otherwise excellent trades. You'll deteriorate winning trades by holding too long, attempting to eject a couple of more pips, and after that enjoying the marketplace break you. And experience larger losses when you let your losses run, or perhaps increase the size of losing positions in an effort to make back your losses

Absence of discipline weakens consistency. If you double your cash in a month, however then lose 70% the following month since you didn't follow your method, you're down 40%.

How come you lost cash the next month? If this is a repeating circumstance, then I 'd state that an absence of discipline triggered you to lose cash.

If your system is working for one month and not the next. You begin making spontaneous trades, simply based on gut-feeling. This is the minute you lose.

Having the discipline to manage your favourable feelings, in addition to your unfavourable feelings, is essential. As excessive self-confidence can result in your failure.

" When you get overconfident, that's when something grabs and bites you." I'm speaking from individual experience. Here's a spontaneous trade I just recently made that expense me significantly.

I 'd been viewing an in proportion triangle development and had actually set a stop order (red line in the diagram) listed below the triangle in order to take advantage of a downwards breakout.

The marketplace did undoubtedly breakout listed below the triangle, my stop order was set off, and I got in a brief position at 7532.01.

Soon later on, I discovered that the Stochastic indication on my chart was revealing that the marketplace was oversold, and may increase! I 'd experienced a string of losses prior to this point, so I was being rather protective and chose to close my brief position practically instantly at 7493.83 (dotted green line).

As you can see from the chart below, the rate dropped to a low of 6450.00. I lost out on relocation of over $1,000! Due to the fact that I made a spontaneous choice AFTER I 'd opened a position and all.

After the training, things began to enhance significantly.

"Behavioural trading has to do with turning the spotlight back on yourself and making good sense what is taking place for you.".

Behavioural trading has to do with turning the spotlight back on yourself and making good sense what is occurring for you.

The training had actually held up a metaphorical mirror which for the very first time permitted me to see myself not as I wished to see myself, however as other would see me.-- This was extremely empowering.

Behavioural trading is the concept that success comes not from understanding where or what to offer or purchase, however, to how 'to be' when purchasing, offering and handling your threat.

Trading psychology is an observational evaluation of what individuals have taken part in trading is doing from a mental point of view.

A few of the very best traders I deal with continuously groan about their absence of discipline, yet they are extremely pleased when their inklings lead them on to act upon a news occasion which ends up being the trade of the year.-- In fact, discipline would never have required them to take on that trade.

Psychology And Mindset

Total financier belief regularly drives market efficiency in instructions that are at chances with the principles.

The effective financier controls fear and greed, the two human feelings that drive that belief.

Comprehending this can offer you the discipline and neutrality required to benefit from others' feelings.

Comprehending Fear

They naturally get frightened when traders get bad news about a particular stock or about the economy in basic. They might feel and overreact obliged to liquidate their holdings and rest on the money, avoiding taking any more dangers. They might prevent particular losses however might likewise miss out on out on some gains if they do.

Traders require to comprehend what worry is: a natural response to a viewed danger. In this case, it's a danger to their revenue capacity.

- ✓ Understanding can likewise assist conquer worry.

- ✓ There are two primary feelings to keep and comprehend under control: worry and greed.

Traders ought to occasionally evaluate their own efficiencies. In addition to evaluating their returns and private positions, traders must assess how they got ready for a trading session, how as much as the date they are on the marketplaces, and how they're advancing in regards to continuous education. This regular evaluation can assist appropriate trader errors, bad modification practices, and boost total returns.

Setting Rules

When the mental crunch comes, a trader requires to produce guidelines and follow them. When to get in a trade and when to leave it, set out standards based on your risk-reward tolerance for. Set a revenue target and put a stop loss in location to take feeling out of the procedure.

Greed is hard to get rid of. It's frequently based upon the impulse to do much better, to get simply a bit more. A trader must discover to acknowledge this impulse and establish a trading strategy based upon logical thinking, not impulses or impulses.

Performing Research and Review

Traders require to end up being specialists in the stocks and markets that intrigue them. Keep top of the news, inform yourself and, if possible, go to trading workshops and go to conferences.

It's a good idea to set limitations on the optimum quantity you want to lose or win in a day. Take the cash and run if you struck the earnings target. Fold up your camping tent and go house if your losses struck an established number.

Including feeling, believing rapidly, and working out discipline are elements of what we may call trading psychology.

In addition, you may choose which particular occasions, such as an unfavourable or favourable profits release, must activate a choice to offer stock or purchase.

Snap Decisions

Traders typically have to believe quick and make fast choices, darting in and out of stocks on brief notification. They likewise require the discipline to stick with their own trading strategies and understand when to reserve losses and earnings.

Conquering Greed

There's an old stating on Wall Street that "pigs get butchered." This describes the practice greedy financiers have of holding on to a winning position too long to get every last tick up in cost. Eventually, the pattern reverses, and the greedy get captured.

In any case, you'll live to trade another day.

Dedicate as much time as possible to the research study procedure. That implies studying charts, talking to management, checking out trade journals, and doing other background work such as macroeconomic analysis or market analysis.

Carrying Out Research and Review

Numerous abilities are needed for trading effectively in the monetary markets. They consist of the capabilities to examine a business's basics and to identify the instructions of a stock's pattern. Neither of these technical abilities is as crucial as the trader's state of mind.

Worry and greed are the two visceral feelings to keep in control.

By believing it through ahead of time, traders will understand how they view occasions intuitively and respond to them, and can move past the psychological action. Naturally, this is hard. However, it's required to the health of a financier's portfolio, not to discuss the financier.

Measuring the worry may assist. Traders ought to think about simply what they hesitate of, and why they hesitate of it. That thinking must take place prior to the bad news, not in the middle of it

Stay Flexible

It's crucial for traders to stay versatile and think about exploring from time to time. One of the finest methods a trader can find out is by exploring (within factor)

RISK AND ACCOUNT MANAGEMENT

No day trader is ideal, and all-day traders will undoubtedly have losing trades. A day trader can have a 50% win rate and still be successful if they're typical revenue is two times the quantity of their typical loss. Contrarily, another trader might have a 75% win rate with typical losses that are four times greater than their typical earnings.

Long-Term Profitability Formula

This formula can be utilized to identify a trader's long-lasting success.

Utilizing this formula, let's compare the result of 2 various traders who each location 10 trades:

Trader A.

- ✓ 50% Win Rate.

- ✓ 50% Loss Rate.
- ✓ $ 200 Average Profit.
- ✓ $ 100 Average Loss.
- ✓ 10= $500 Profit.

Trader B.

- ✓ 75% Win Rate.
- ✓ 25% Loss Rate.
- ✓ $ 100 Average Profit.
- ✓ $ 400 Average Loss.
- ✓ 10= -$ 250 Loss.

Risk/Reward Ratios.

Effective day traders are typically conscious of both the prospective risk and possible benefit prior to getting in a trade. The objective of a day trader is to put trades where the prospective benefit exceeds the possible risk. If you believe a prospective trade might result in either a $400 revenue or $100 loss, the trade would have a risk/reward ratio of 4:1, making it a beneficial setup.

With concerns to the long-lasting success formula above, discovering trades with high risk/reward ratios (3:1 or greater) will assist you to keep greater typical earnings and lower typical losses, making your trading technique more sustainable.

Although Trader B has a greater win rate, he is not successful due to a bad risk management technique. What is the point of this? Restricting losses is simply as important as increasing your win rate and, normally speaking, and it is a lot easier to restrict losses than it is to increase your win rate.

Cutting Losses.

Stopping out of a losing trade can be one of the hardest things for day traders to do regularly. Stopping working to take stops can result in margin calls, needlessly big losses, and eventually account blowouts.

Risk Reward Ratios.

Greater risk/reward ratios offer traders an edge in the marketplaces.

TECHNICAL ANALYSIS

A day trader who can acknowledge a pattern on the charts can figure out where costs are probably to go up until some unpredicted occasion occurs that produces a brand-new pattern. Technical analysis is the tool that assists a day trader to identify those patterns.

Technical analysis is the research study of previous market information to anticipate the instructions of future rate motions. Along with simple research, the method is conceived of as a branch of protection research. Here we look at how technological modelling can be seen in day-trading.

In a lot of markets, every day produces a brand-new bar (lots of traders discuss bars rather of days, and they aren't discussing where they pursue work). A collection of bars, with all their various high, low, open, and close points, is created into a bigger chart. Typically, a plot of the volume for each bar runs beneath.

Numerous patterns formed in the charts are connected with future rate relocations. Technical experts, therefore, invest a great deal of time taking a look at the charts to see whether they can anticipate what is going to occur. When particular technical patterns take place so that the traders can position orders appropriately, lots of software application plans send out traders signals.

The plots form patterns that can be examined to reveal what occurred. How did the supply and need for a security modification, and why? And what does that mean for future supply and need?

A couple of market individuals want to go that far. However, they yield the point that the rate is the single essential summary of details about a business. That suggests that technical analysis, taking a look at how the rate modifications in time, is a method of discovering whether a security's potential customers are enhancing or becoming worse.

1. Presumptions in Technical Analysis

While some financiers and traders utilize both technical and basic analysis, most tend to fall under one camp or another or a minimum of depending on one much more greatly in making trading choices.

Macro-level basic analysis requires the research study or forecasting of financial development, inflation, credit cycles, rates of interest patterns, capital circulations in between nations, labour and resource usage and their cyclicality, market patterns, reserve bank and political policies and habits, geopolitical matters, customer and organisation patterns, and "soft" information (e.g., belief or self-confidence studies).

Many big banks and brokerages have groups that focus on both technical and essential analysis. In basic, the more quality details one takes in to enhance the chances of being right, the much better one's trading outcomes are most likely to be.

Technical analysis is based upon the property that securities rates relocate patterns which those patterns duplicate themselves in time. Details about the cost, time, and volume of a security's trading can be outlined on a chart.

It frequently contrasts with basic analysis, which can be used both on a macroeconomic and microeconomic level. The micro-level essential analysis consists of the research study of incomes, expenses, liabilities, possessions and revenues, capital structure, and "soft" aspects (quality of management group, competitive position).

The standard component of technical analysis is a bar, which reveals you the high, low, open, and closing cost of security for an offered day.

Technical analysis is a method to determine the supply and need in the market. It's a tool for evaluating the marketplaces, not forecasting them. Everybody would be able to make cash in the markets if analyzing the significance of the information were that simple.

2. Volume modifications

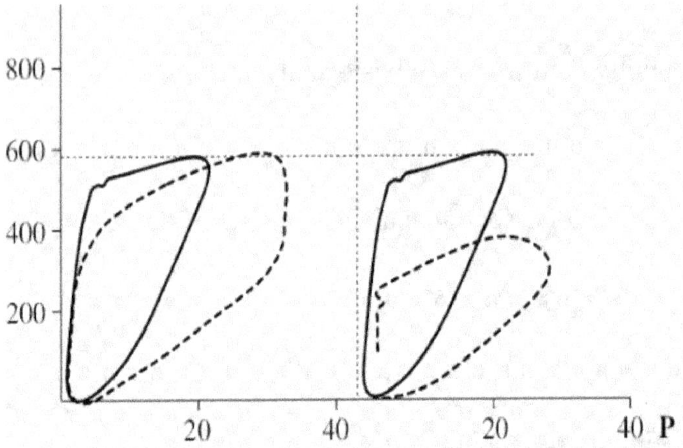

The standard bar demonstrates how rate altered throughout the day, however including volume details informs the other part of the story: just how much of security was required at that cost. If the need is increasing, then more individuals desire security, so they want to pay more for it. The rate informs traders what the marketplace understands;

the volume informs them the number of individuals in the market understands it.

3. Cost modifications

Changes to home flooring	21,850	0	1,900 (8.7%)	11,950 (53.8%)	6,000 (27.5%)	1,561
Door Widening	34,408	1,775 (5.2%)	17,431 (50.7%)	7,426 (21.6%)	7,776 (22.6%)	1,911
Electric bed	33,407	13,264 (39.7%)	5,350 (16.0%)	9,550 (28.6%)	5,243 (15.7%)	1,758
Hand rail & Grab rail	1,277	290 (22.7%)	697 (54.6%)	0	290 (22.7%)	256
Hoist	32,000	5,600 (17.5%)	25,600 (80%)	0	800 (2.5%)	1,684
Ramps	76,933	4,433 (5.8%)	49,967 (64.9%)	18,000 (23.4%)	4,533 (5.9%)	2,564
Specialized Mattress	9,400	5,400 (57.4%)	600 (6.4%)	2,800 (29.8%)	600 (6.4%)	627
Stair Lift	5,985	1,500 (37.5%)	995 (24.9%)	1,500 (37.5%)	0	1,197
Stair rail	785	327 (41.7%)	131 (16.7%)	262 (33.4%)	65 (8.3%)	65
Extensive home improvement	199,000	0	143,000 (71.9%)	11,000 (5.5%)	45,000 (22.5%)	33,166

Market observers argument market performance all the time. In an effective market, all info about security is currently consisted of in the security's cost, so there's no indicate doing any research study at all.

4. Market Cyclicality

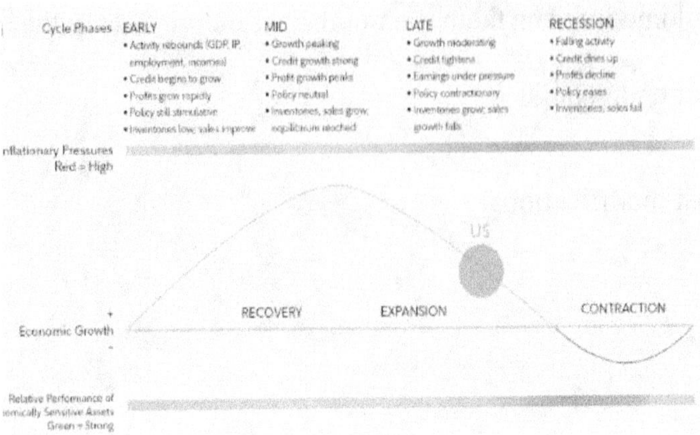

Humanity being what it is, with typically shared behavioural attributes, market history tends to duplicate itself. The series of occasions is not apt to duplicate itself completely. However, the patterns are usually comparable. These can take the kind of short-term or long-lasting rate habits.

Another presumption behind technical analysis (and all securities analysis more broadly) is that cost does stagnate according to a "random walk", or according to no rational or noticeable pattern. Rather it moves according to patterns that are both foreseeable and explainable.

Technical analysis alone can not completely or properly anticipate the future; it is beneficial to recognize patterns, behavioural predispositions, and prospective inequalities in supply and need where trading chances might develop.

5. Analytical Approaches

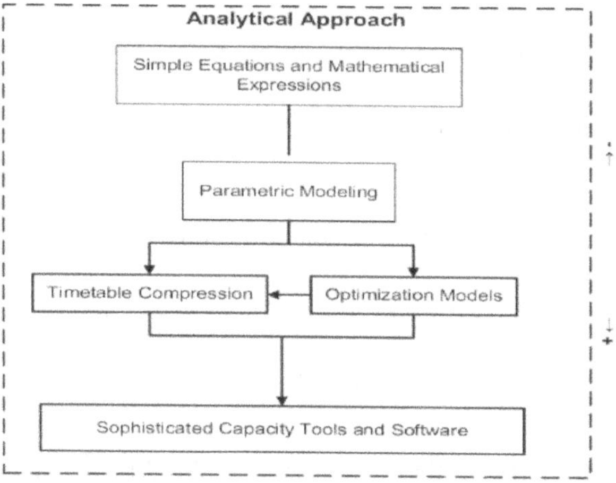

There are numerous methods to approach technical analysis. The most basic technique is through a fundamental candlestick cost chart, which reveals cost history and the purchasing and offering characteristics of cost within a given duration.

Initially, technical analysis was mainly a matter of "checking out the tape" or analyzing the succeeding circulation and magnitude of cost and volume information through a stock ticker. As computer systems ended up being more extensive in the 1970s, information was assembled into chart kind and ended up being a service technician's basic point of recommendation.

Acknowledgement of chart patterns and bar (or later on candlestick) analysis were the most typical kinds of analysis, followed by regression analysis, moving averages, and rate connections. Today, the variety of technical signs are far more many. Anybody with coding understanding appropriate to the software application can change rate or volume information into a specific indication of interest.

Others use a cost chart together with technical indications or utilize specific kinds of technical analysis, such as Elliott wave theory or harmonics, to produce trade concepts. Some usage parts of a number of various approaches. At the exact same time, traders need to withstand the concept of "details overload" or jumbling charts with numerous signs and lines that it starts to negatively affect one's capability to check out the chart.

6. Candlestick

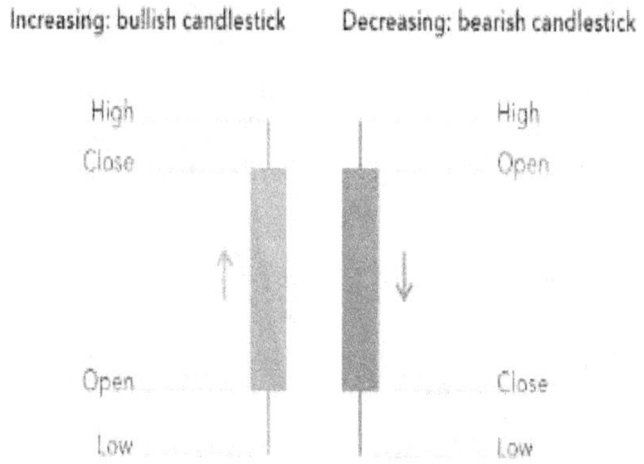

Candlestick charts are the most typical type of charting in today's software application. Green (or in some cases white) is typically utilized to illustrate bullish candle lights, where the existing rate is greater than the opening cost. Red (or often black) prevails for bearish candle lights, where present cost is listed below the opening cost.

When particular guidelines evenly use to enhance the neutrality of their trading and prevent psychological predispositions from affecting its efficiency, others might get in into trades just.

Traders might take a subjective judgment to their trading calls, preventing the requirement to trade based upon a limiting rules-based technique provided the originality of each circumstance.

Overlay indications are positioned over the initial rate chart.

Moving Average-- A pattern line that alters based upon brand-new cost inputs. A 50-day basic moving average would represent the typical cost of the previous 50 trading days. Rapid moving averages weight the line more greatly towards current rates.

7. Non-Chart Based.

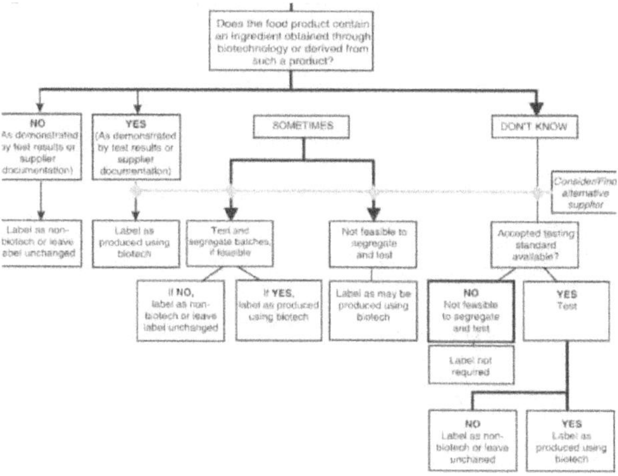

Not all technical analysis is based upon charting or arithmetical improvements of cost. Some technical experts depend on sentiment-based studies from organisations and customers to assess where the rate may be going.

Heiken-Ashi charts utilize candlesticks as the outlining medium, however, take the various mathematical formula of cost. Rather of the guideline of candle lights equated from standard open-high-low-close requirements, rates are smoothed to much better show trending cost action according to this formula.

Breakout-- When cost breaches a location of assistance or resistance, frequently due to a significant rise in offering or purchasing volume.

It reveals the range in between the opening and closing costs (the body of the candlelight) and the overall day-to-day variety (from top of the wick to bottom of the wick).

Rate action-- The motion of rate, as graphically represented through a chart of a specific market.

8. Line chart.

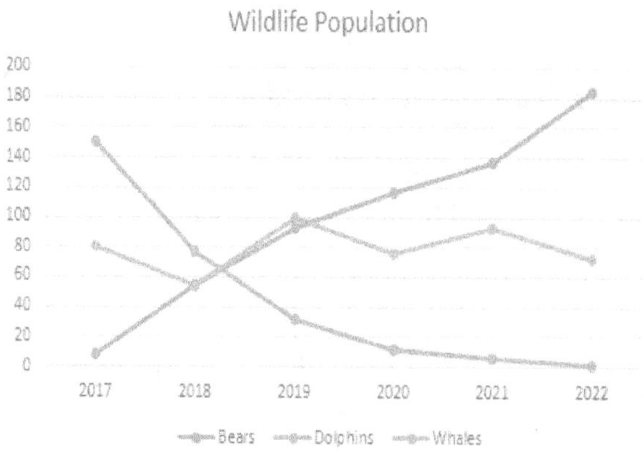

Pattern-- Price motion that continues one instruction for an extended time period.

Resistance-- A rating level where a prevalence of sell orders might lie, triggering cost to bounce off the level downward. Enough purchasing activity, typically from increased volume, is typically needed to breach it.

Bollinger Bands-- Uses a basic moving typical and plots two lines two basic discrepancies above and listed below it to form a variety. Frequently utilized by traders utilizing a mean reversion technique where rate moving above or listed below the bands is "extended" and possibly anticipated to revert back inside the bands.

Ichimoku Cloud-- Designed to be an "all-in-one" sign that offers assistance and resistance, momentum, pattern, and creates trading signals.

If the market is exceptionally bullish, this may be taken as an indication that nearly everybody is totally invested and a couple of purchasers stay on the sidelines to press rates up even more. This may recommend that costs are more likely to trend down.

Favourable Volume Index-- Typically utilized along with the unfavourable volume index, the indication is created to reveal when institutional financiers are most active under the facility they're probably to offer or purchase when the volume is low. When volume is up from the previous day, focuses on days.

On-Balance Volume-- Uses volume to anticipate subsequent modifications in rate. Advocates of the sign location credence into the concept that if volume modifications with a weak response in the stock, the cost relocation is most likely to follow.

Advance-Decline Line-- Measures the number of stocks advanced (gotten in worth) in an index vs the variety of stocks that decreased (declined). If an index has actually gotten in worth, however just 30% of the stocks are up however 70% are down or neutral, that's an indicator that the purchasing is most likely just taking place in particular sectors instead of being favourable towards the whole market.

Product Channel Index (CCI)-- Identifies cyclical conditions or brand-new patterns.

Momentum-- The rate of modification in rate with regard to time.

Retracement-- A turnaround in the instructions of the dominating pattern, anticipated to be short-term, typically to a level of assistance or resistance.

Doji-- A candlelight type defined by little or no modification in between the close and open rate, revealing indecision in the market.

Stochastic Oscillator-- Shows the present rate of the security or index relative to the low and high rates from a user-defined variety. They were utilized to identify overbought and oversold market conditions.

Channel-- Two parallel pattern lines set to imagine a combination pattern of specific instructions. A breakout above or listed below a channel might be translated as an indication of a possible trading and a brand-new pattern chance.

Momentum-- The rate of modification of cost with regard to time.

Typical Directional Movement Rating (ADXR)-- Measures the rate of modification in a pattern.

A worth listed below one is thought about bullish; a worth above one is thought about bearish. Volume is determined in the variety of shares traded and not the dollar quantities, which is a main defect in the sign (prefers lower price-per-share stocks, which can sell greater volume). It is however still shown on the flooring of the New York Stock Exchange. (of advancing stocks/ of decreasing stocks)/ (volume of advancing stocks/ volume of decreasing stocks).

Arms Index (aka TRIN)-- Combines the variety of stocks decreasing or advancing with their volume according to the formula.

Coppock Curve-- Momentum indication, at first meant to recognize bottoms in stock indices as part of a long-lasting trading technique.

9. Volume-based.

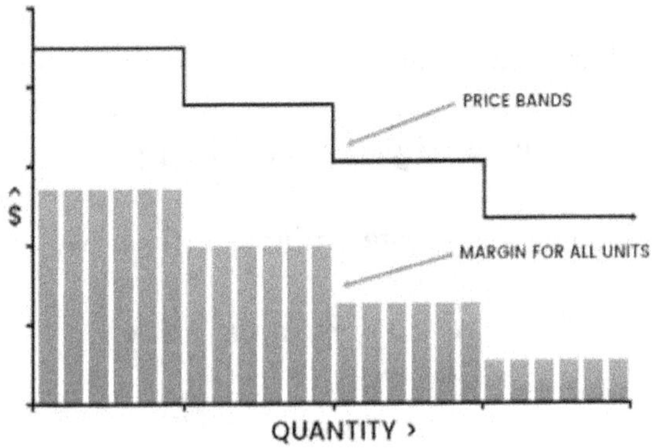

Cash Flow Index-- Measures the circulation of cash into and out of stock over a specific duration.

Moving Average-- A weighted average of rates to show the pattern over a series of worths.

Williams Accumulation/Distribution-- Looks at divergences in between security (or index) cost and volume circulation. When traders are collecting (purchasing) or distributing (selling), this is developed to figure out. When rate makes a brand-new low, and the sign stops working to likewise make a brand-new low, this may be taken as an indicator that build-up (purchasing) is happening.

If 98% of the stocks are up however just 2% are down or neutral at the open of the marketplace, it's an indicator that the marketplace may be more trendless and "reversion to the mean" day trading methods might be more efficient. If an uneven advance/decline continues, it might indicate that the market might be trending.

Pivot Points-- Levels of assistance and resistance figured out from the other day's open, high, close and low. They were normally utilized by day traders to discover possible turnaround levels in the market.

Relative Strength Index (RSI)-- Momentum oscillator standardized to a 0-100 scale created to figure out the rate of modification over a defined period.

MACD-- Plots the relationship in between 2 different moving averages; created as a momentum-following indication.

Technical signs include some arithmetical or analytical change of cost and/or volume information to offer mathematical descriptions of up/down motion, assistance and resistance levels, momentum, pattern, discrepancies from the main propensity, ratio(s), connection(s), to name a few delineations. Some indications likewise explain a belief, such as brief interest, suggested volatility, put/call ratios, "worry" or "greed", etc.

Supporters of the theory state that when one of the patterns in specific instructions, the other is most likely to follow. A high volume of products deliveries and deals is a sign that the economy is on a sound footing.

Unfavourable Volume Index-- Designed to comprehend when the "wise cash" is active, under the presumption that the wise cash is most active on low-volume days and not as active on high-volume days. When volume is down from the previous day, indication focuses on the day-to-day level.

10. Breadth.

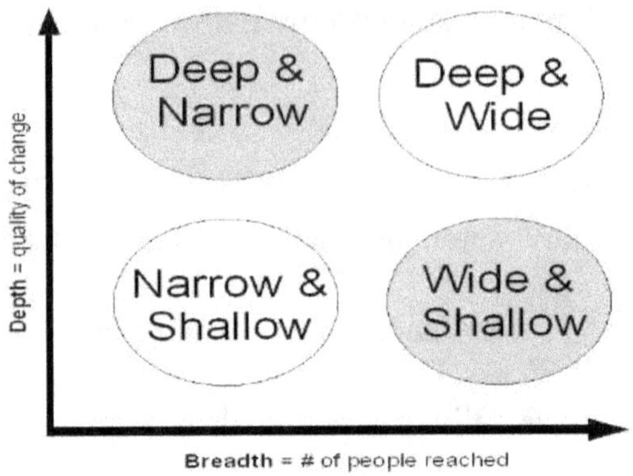

Change projects: Possible results

Breadth signs identify how strong or shallow a market relocation is.

Fibonacci Lines A tool for assistance and resistance normally developed by outlining the sign from the low and high of a current pattern.

Typical real variety-- The variety over a particular period, generally daily.

Parabolic SAR-- Intended to discover short-term turnaround patterns in the market. Usually just suggested for trending markets.

Cycle-- Periods where rate action is anticipated to follow a specific pattern.

11. Line.

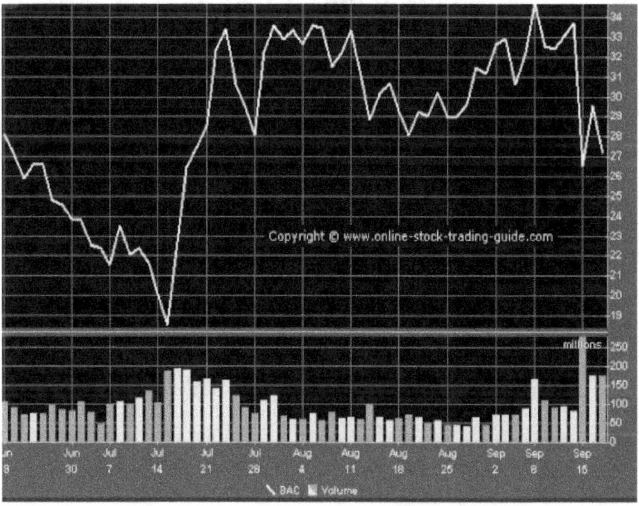

A line chart links information points utilizing a line, typically from the closing cost of each period.

Assistance-- A cost level where a greater magnitude of buy orders might be put, triggering rate to bounce off the level up. If there is adequate selling activity surpassing purchasing activity, the level will not hold.

Fibonacci ratios-- Numbers utilized as a guide to identifying assistance and resistance.

Pattern line-- A sloped line formed from 2 or more peaks or troughs on the rate chart. A break above or listed below a pattern line may be a sign of a breakout.

12. Open-High Low-Close.

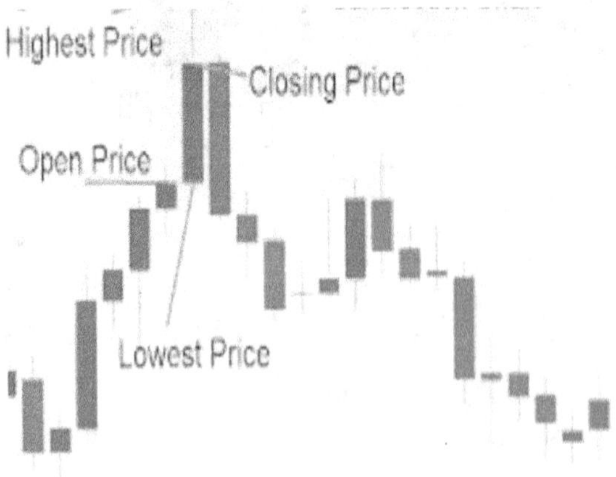

A candlestick chart resembles an open-high-low-close chart, likewise referred to as a bar chart. Rather of the body of the candlelight revealing the distinction in between the close and open cost, these levels are represented by horizontal tick marks. The opening cost tick points to the left (to reveal that it came from the past) while the other cost tick points to the.

Elliott wave theory-- Elliott wave theory recommends that markets go through cyclical durations of optimism and pessimism that can be anticipated and therefore ripe for trading chances.

Harmonics-- Harmonic trading is based upon the concept that cost patterns duplicate themselves and turning points in the market can be determined through Fibonacci series.

Finest utilized when cost and the oscillator are diverging. When cost is making a brand-new low; however, the oscillator is making a brand-new high, this might represent a purchasing chance.

A location chart is basically the like a line chart, with the location under it shaded. This is primarily done to more quickly picture the cost motion relative to a line chart.

Dead feline bounce-- When cost decreases in a down market, there might be an uptick in rate where purchasers are available in thinking the possession is low-cost or offering exaggerated. When sellers require the market down even more, the short-lived purchasing spell comes to be understood as a dead feline bounce.

- ✓ Open = (Open of previous bar + Close of previous bar)/ 2.
- ✓ Close = (Open + Low + high + Close)/ 4.
- ✓ High = Highest of High, Open, or Close.

- ✓ Low = Lowest of Low, Open, or Close.
- ✓ Heiken Ashi chart.

Technical signs fall under a couple of primary classifications, consisting of price-based, volume-based, breadth, overlays, and non-chart based.

Typical Directional Index (ADX)-- Measures pattern strength on an outright worth basis.

MISTAKES TO AVOID ON DAY TRADING

You require to end up being familiar with some typical errors that lead to failure for lots of day traders if the expenses and threats do not terrify you away from day trading. Here are a few of the more major errors brand-new day traders make:

The worst sensation, even for a knowledgeable trader, takes place when a stock plunges far listed below the stop position since choosing whether to take a big loss is challenging. If you're unpredictable of your next relocation, experienced traders suggest that you get out of the position prior to the scenario grows even worse or out of control.

By missing out on desired entry costs, traders wind up chasing after the patterns and discovering that their initial entry and exit points no longer stand.

You likewise might wish to think about taking your Series 7 test, the test all stockbrokers are needed to pass. You should be sponsored to take the examination, numerous training centres near your house or online can assist you to discover a sponsoring broker.

Even prior to you start, make certain to take a look at the companies you're preparing to utilize as resources by calling their disciplinary records and problem histories through the SEC or state regulators. You're putting a bargain of cash at danger, so put in the time to learn all you can previously investing even that very first penny.

Not waiting on the best trade: A brand-new day trader should show the perseverance needed in waiting on the best trade to match what the technical analysis suggests. Experienced traders understand to wait on the ideal timing rather of requiring a trade, going into at the incorrect rate, and overtrading their account.

Experienced day traders understand that you either concentrate on your trades or think of your guidelines. Do not do both. Remaining goal and following your guidelines is important to keeping the control a day trader requirements.

Breaking stop-loss guidelines: When a stock begins dropping, more recent, not-yet-disciplined traders tend to worry as their choices start losing cash, so they choose to hold the stock instead of exit when their preliminary stop-loss is reached. Traders go broke utilizing that technique. Follow those guidelines mechanically when the target cost is struck, and do not let your feelings obstruct.

Day trading is a high-risk profession option that you ought to think about just after doing a significant quantity of preliminary research study, searching down great resources for informing yourself about the benefits and dangers and discovering all the strategies you require to utilize to day trade effectively.

Not developing set guidelines prior to the trading day starts: To prevent getting captured up in the feelings of a big win or loss, you require to choose your entry and exit points prior to the trading day starts and never ever differ them after the day starts.

A lot of brand-new traders are attracted by the possibility to make big amounts of cash in the stock market. This kind of enjoyment can be a terrific incentive for brand-new traders. Nevertheless, it can likewise trigger them to make some rash, unreasonable choices. If you desire to end up being an effective day trader, you require to put in the hours and work for it.

Doing so offers you time to look objectively at what is occurring with the stock and identify whether returning in is beneficial. Stopping out likewise is most likely to cost you less than balancing down, and you will not run the risk of getting captured with a margin issue. Balancing down can bind excessive cash that otherwise can be utilized for a more rewarding trade with various stock.

Not understanding when to take revenues: New traders in some cases make the error of either taking earnings prematurely or not taking revenues at all. The majority of the time, indecision strikes when traders hesitate they'll lose earnings if they hold it too long or miss out on revenue if they leave prematurely. Exit points require to be identified prior to going into a position, and guidelines require to be followed.

Despite the fact that you might never ever wish to work as a broker, the info you're needed to understand for the examination provides you with a much more powerful awareness of the securities markets and the laws by which they're governed. Studying for the test, you'll likewise find more about the numerous financial investment items on the marketplace and the dangers you take when offering each type and purchasing.

Bear in mind that as a day trader, you need to focus either on your trade or on your guidelines. Day traders who move into and out of positions within minutes or seconds do not have time to do both.

Ignoring the computer system with employment opportunities: Experienced day traders never ever leave their computer systems when they still have an employment opportunity. They certainly do not desire to be away from the screen while a position is still open due to the fact that knowledgeable day traders react to price modifications that take place in simple seconds or minutes.

Experienced traders understand that how great the principles look does not matter which when the marketplace is offering down, even the rate of a great stock decreases. Day traders should follow market indications and not fret about how great or bad the principles of the business they're trading might appear.

Balancing down: Although financiers might balance down, implying they purchase a stock and if the cost decreases they purchase more shares thinking that it will recuperate, this method does not operate at all for day traders, and many knowledgeable traders will inform you that utilizing it is a deadly error. Day traders rather think that you require to set a stop rate and leave a losing stock.

Forgetting that basics do not matter: New day traders get captured up in the concept that the business whose stock they've bought is an excellent business which when its stock loses ground, it's for that reason bound to head back up.

When we have brand-new traders approach us about getting begun with trading, we constantly advise our DVD's. We suggest that brand-new traders enjoy the DVDs so that they can come to the market positive and ready. Going into the market, unprepared is lots of, and really dangerous traders blow up their accounts due to their hastiness.

I have actually been running Investors Underground for a long period of time now and trading for even longer. I typically see brand-new traders duplicate the very same errors. I wish to assist you to prevent making these errors so that you can have the very best chance at success.

1. Entering Unprepared

As pointed out above, trading stocks need to not show betting. You require to inform yourself about trading so that you are correctly geared up to master the stock market. You require to understand how the market works, what kinds of setups you are looking for, and why, and how you will respond in a trade.

Going after patterns: New traders typically wait to see verification that they're ideal prior to they get in a position. That doubt triggers them to miss out on scheduled entry points and, if they're right, can wind up requiring them into purchasing a stock rate that's greater than they meant when an upward pattern is anticipated or costing a lower cost than they planned when a down pattern is anticipated.

2. Absence of Proper Tools

Trading is an art, and simply like any craft, it needs the correct tools and resources. Make sure your tool kit is properly provided prior to you embark on your trading journey. Do your research study and make sure you have what you require to correctly perform your trading strategy.

3. Entering Too Big

You will typically see lots of parallels in between brand-new traders and bettors since the stock market and the gambling establishment both have a comparable appeal. A lot of individuals understand that they have extremely low chances in the gambling establishment. Nevertheless, not numerous individuals understand that they have comparable changes in the stock market if they take the incorrect method.

Cash management is simply as essential as a trading method since it assists your secure your capital. Even a trader with a 90% win rate stands an opportunity of blowing up their account if they go all in. It might sting a bit to feel like you might have made more on trade; however, it will sting considerably more difficult if you blow up your trading account and take yourself out of the video game.

4. Following vs Learning

When individuals get begun in trading, they frequently look for a coach to discover. It's terrific to discover from the successes and failures of a knowledgeable trader. They draw in traders who just desire to copy the specific trades of an effective trader.

5. Balancing Down

One of the worst errors brand-new traders make is balancing down. No one likes to take losses; however, taking a little loss is much better than getting yourself in a position where you can be taken out of the trading video game. There will be plenty of other trading chances if you protect your capital.

6. Not Cutting Losses

As discussed in the past, no one likes taking losses. However, it is an essential part of the video game. You require to understand how much cash you are ready to run the risk of on a play and then follow through with it. If you ever lose more than that, you broke your trading guidelines.

7. Revenge Trading

There's absolutely nothing even worse than attempting to make up for a bad trade by putting more trades. You need to just trade when you have a strong trading and a prime setup strategy. You do not have to keep trading.

How To Increase Your Chances Of Success – Golden Rules Of Trading

Trading needs to be dealt with in a really expert way precisely like a company where you keep a close watch on all losses, tax worths, tension levels and run the risk of management. Make certain to prepare ahead and treat this as major as possible.

Mastering these develop strong impulses that will direct you much better in trading needs to be dealt with in a really expert way precisely like a company where you keep a close watch on all

losses, tax worths, tension levels and run the risk of management. Make certain to prepare ahead and treat this as major as possible.

Mastering these develop strong impulses that will direct you much better in the universe of comprehending how trading subtleties work, how world politics really work, how occasions come to affect the trading cross in the chart and most crucial the speed of the international economies. Attempt to comprehend that nearly every occasion has an effect on the trading cross.

1: Never hesitate to utilize a Stop Loss

Trading constantly includes a lot of dangers; this is why the stop loss action has actually been developed so you can retreat from losing funds which can be an entire amount of cash or a specific portion. Both procedures operate in the exact same way and have the sole goal to restrict the losses throughout a stopped working trade. By utilizing a stop loss, you can secure yourself from losing a great deal of cash.

If you disregard a stop loss alert, even if it ends up being effective, this is a really bad practice to get utilized to. Leaving the trading premises with a stop-loss action even if this indicates losing to the procedure is still an advantage since you have actually handled to prevent losing cash totally and can get back at them with much better positions on the trading chart. Constantly secure yourself with all the steps that you have at your disposal.

2: Trade with truths, not fiction

Among the most crucial guidelines of being an effective trader is to constantly take your time in establishing the perfect trading technique finest matched for you due to the fact that it is absolutely worth the effort. Constantly utilize truths when developing your method, never ever utilize feelings, shy hopes or magnificent powers since mysticism does not work here. Here you handle cold mathematical strong truths.

Nowadays being an effective trader suggests having an efficient and strong trading system with crystal clear objectives and a tough set of trading guidelines of increasing your possibility of success. It is really an effective trader is far from simple, however in the Forex world of trading, being effective ways transferring a considerable quantity of cash in your bank account and everybody begins its journey from a shoreline. This needs establishing a strong trading technique in accordance with your threat tolerance and monetary target.

3: Protect Your Trading Capital

Keeping your expenditures short has actually never ever been simple; however, this is precisely what you require to do in order to preserve a brand-new trading account. This is really the entire concept of the trading procedure in the Forex world to have as little stops working as possible and more wins. By safeguarding your account, you really prevent taking unneeded threats and release rather an all-out effort in keeping your trading and making the procedure smooth and simple.

Numerous trading platforms use the needed innovation to expect whether your next relocation will be bad or great. Evaluating a trading concept prior to running the risk of genuine cash is now a reality worth accepting and eventually including to your trading strategy.

4: First establish your really own Trading Plan

A trading strategy is a particular set of hand composed guidelines for you to follow without a doubt and regard it with military discipline. By making usage of a trading strategy, you can rapidly manage your financial investments and handle your losses to keep them as low as possible.

5: Always keep your dangers low in accordance with what you can pay for to lose

Positioning funds in your account brings excellent obligation which action needs you to be conscious of all your trading actions of buy or sell. We truthfully advise you to constantly start trading with a demonstration account to get a genuine feel of the trading market and dive to trading with genuine cash just when you feel great sufficient to leap in the field.

6: Always study the motion of the Forex markets

Picture this guideline to be an endless class that you need to handle a day-to-day basis in which you continuously find out brand-new things all the time no exceptions enabled. Worldwide of Forex details is power and understanding is strength for that reason traders are needed to continue finding out day-to-day and remain as notified as possible with all the adjustments on the trading chart.

Traders should have a strong, stoic discipline when it concerns handling cash, and sometimes you need to be emotionally prepared to lose a part of your cash from your trading account. Traders who make a great deal of cash likewise require to find out how to act. When you are on a gaining spree, you taste sweet success and can be seduced into delving into trading choices without believing it out completely.

7: Manage your trading efforts like a genuine service

Lots of stop working from the start due to the fact that they make the error of thinking that trading is a pastime and not an occupation, whereas success comes the other method around. Do not deal with the trading procedure like a task since it is going to end up being really aggravating really quick as the income is irregular.

On the very same page, we can discover that a winning trade is just a little action towards your objective in changing your trading into constant revenues. Typically feelings require to sit this one out as the total trading efficiency is impacted considerably by it.

8: Never stop trading even when things spoil

Constantly keep your efforts and wits focused on the huge image. In other words, constantly keep your eyes on the reward.

The Forex market can be really unpredictable at times, and lots of traders lose a lot of cash actually quickly, the reality is informed. You should keep your costs short due to the fact that the statement "you have to invest cash to make cash" is not real. No trader is 100% effective.

A stop-loss order is a basic tool, yet numerous financiers stop working to utilize it. Whether to avoid extreme losses or to secure earnings, almost all investing designs can gain from this trade. Consider a stop loss as an insurance coverage: you hope you never ever need to utilize it. However, it's excellent to understand you have the security must you require it. The universe of comprehending how trading subtleties work, how world politics really work, how occasions come to affect the trading cross in the chart and most crucial the speed of the international economies. Attempt to comprehend that nearly every occasion has an effect on the trading cross.

9: Never hesitate to utilize a Stop Loss

Trading constantly includes a lot of dangers; this is why the stop loss action has actually been developed so you can retreat from losing funds which can be an entire amount of cash or a specific portion. Both procedures operate in the exact same way and have the sole goal to restrict the losses throughout a stopped working trade. By utilizing a stop loss, you can secure yourself from losing a great deal of cash.

If you disregard a stop loss alert, even if it ends up being effective, this is a really bad practice to get utilized to. Leaving the trading premises with a stop-loss action even if this indicates losing to the procedure is still an advantage since you have actually handled to prevent losing cash totally and can get back at them with much better positions on the trading chart. Constantly secure yourself with all the steps that you have at your disposal.

10: Trade with truths, not fiction

Among the most crucial guidelines of being an effective trader is to constantly take your time in establishing the perfect trading technique finest matched for you due to the fact that it is absolutely worth the effort. Constantly utilize truths when developing your method, never ever utilize feelings, shy hopes or magnificent powers since mysticism does not work here. Here you handle cold mathematical strong truths.

Nowadays being an effective trader suggests having an efficient and strong trading system with crystal clear objectives and a tough set of trading guidelines of increasing your possibility of success. It is really an effective trader is far from simple, however in the Forex world of trading, being effective ways transferring a considerable quantity of cash in your bank account and everybody begins its journey from a shoreline. This needs establishing a strong trading technique in accordance with your threat tolerance and monetary target.

11: Protect Your Trading Capital

Keeping your expenditures short has actually never ever been simple; however, this is precisely what you require to do in order to preserve a brand-new trading account. This is really the entire concept of the trading procedure in the Forex world to have as little stops working as possible and more wins. By safeguarding your account, you really prevent taking unneeded threats and release rather an all-out effort in keeping your trading and making the procedure smooth and simple.

Numerous trading platforms use the needed innovation to expect whether your next relocation will be bad or great. Evaluating a trading concept prior to running the risk of genuine cash is now a reality worth accepting and eventually including to your trading strategy.

12: First establish your really own Trading Plan

A trading strategy is a particular set of hand composed guidelines for you to follow without a doubt and regard it with military discipline. By making usage of a trading strategy, you can rapidly manage your financial investments and handle your losses to keep them as low as possible.

13: Always keep your dangers low in accordance with what you can pay for to lose

Positioning funds in your account brings excellent obligation which action needs you to be conscious of all your trading actions of buy or sell. We truthfully advise you to constantly start trading with a demonstration account to get a genuine feel of the trading market and dive to trading with genuine cash just when you feel great sufficient to leap in the field.

14: Always study the motion of the Forex markets

Picture this guideline to be an endless class that you need to handle a day-to-day basis in which you continuously find out brand-new things all the time no exceptions enabled. Worldwide of Forex details is power and understanding is strength for that reason traders are needed to continue finding out day-to-day and remain as notified as possible with all the adjustments on the trading chart.

Traders should have a strong, stoic discipline when it concerns handling cash, and sometimes you need to be emotionally prepared to lose a part of your cash from your trading account. Traders who make a great deal of cash likewise require to find out how to act. When you are on a gaining spree, you taste sweet success and can be seduced into delving into trading choices without believing it out completely.

15: Manage your trading efforts like a genuine service

Lots of stop working from the start due to the fact that they make the error of thinking that trading is a pastime and not an occupation, whereas success comes the other method around. Do not deal with the trading procedure like a task since it is going to end up being really aggravating really quick as the income is irregular.

On the very same page, we can discover that a winning trade is just a little action towards your objective in changing your trading into constant revenues. Typically feelings require to sit this one out as the total trading efficiency is impacted considerably by it.

16: Never stop trading even when things spoil

Constantly keep your efforts and wits focused on the huge image. In other words, constantly keep your eyes on the reward.

The Forex market can be really unpredictable at times, and lots of traders lose a lot of cash actually quickly, the reality is informed. You should keep your costs short due to the fact that the statement "you have to invest cash to make cash" is not real. No trader is 100% effective.

A stop-loss order is a basic tool, yet numerous financiers stop working to utilize it. Whether to avoid extreme losses or to secure earnings, almost all investing designs can gain from this trade. Consider a stop loss as an insurance coverage: you hope you never ever need to utilize it. However, it's excellent to understand you have the security must you require it.

CONCLUSION

Once again, day trading is not for everybody. However, this book, based upon hard-won, individual experience, provides you with the details you require to see if day trading is an excellent individual option for you on your journey to monetary liberty and security.

This book offers you the type of standard detailed details you've been trying to find to make an educated choice about day trading. Make no error about it; this kind of speculative stock trading is not for everybody. By setting out the procedure you require to go through in a no-nonsense and useful method, you get a clear concept of simply precisely what you'll be entering when you begin day trading.

Far from dissuading or downhearted, this book provides a practical and well-balanced view of what it's like to prepare to day trade, in addition to the truths you'll deal with when you day trade. You get vital pointers on the state of minds you require to embrace, the tools you require to get, crucial strategies effective and reliable day traders utilize, in addition to directions on how to establish your extremely own effective individual day-trading method.

You are looking at the best book if you are a total rookie to day trading and desire the within dope or straight talk about this kind of securities trading. Rather of investing an excessive quantity of time and book area on just how much you can make from day trading, in addition to the monetary liberty you can delight in, this book focuses the majority of its firepower on what you require to understand so you can be successful with day trading.

Do Not Go Yet; One Last Thing To Do

If you enjoyed this book or found it useful, I'd be very grateful if you'd post a short honest review on my book.

Your support does make a difference, and I will read all the reviews personally so I can get your feedback and make this book even better.

Thanks again for your support!

www.ingramcontent.com/pod-product-compliance
Lightning Source LLC
LaVergne TN
LVHW022211200926
848481LV00006B/1924
9798201768614